THE NEXT REVOLUTION IN BRANDING

BECOMING A
KEY PERSON
OF TRUST

KARIN SEBELIN

First edition 2019

ISBN
978-3-00-060652-6 (pbk)
978-3-00-060653-3 (e-bk)

Contents

Acknowledgements

So much went into getting this book in front of you. I am incredibly and deeply grateful to the people who made it possible.

I'd like to say thank you to my followers and friends on social media, to my business contacts and to my readership, who, through reading my articles and books, steadily encouraged me.

Many friends and contacts generously shared their experience, expertise and knowledge with me during the process of writing this book.

I am especially grateful to some experts who have put their efforts into working out their insights in their special fields of expertise and have added value to my book. Thank you, Denise Lee Yohn (topic branding), Mark W Schaefer (topic marketing), and Neal Schaffer (topic influencer marketing).

And I thank these experts, influencers and thought leaders, who have endorsed my book: Dorie Clark, David Aaker, Frank Sonnenberg, and Nir Eyal.

I'd like to say thank you to my beloved family: you always showed great patience with me, continually supporting and motivating me during the hard times, and believing in me and my work.

To my publishing company, thanks for making my book concept come to life.

Thank you, Anthony Puttee and the team at Book Cover Cafe; it was a real pleasure working with you.

Finally, I want to say thank you to my clients, past and present, for giving me your trust and loyalty.

Introduction

Why did I write this book? You could certainly say that there are already many branding books on the market, so why another one? Good question, indeed.

As an expert on trust, I often had the feeling that we don't put enough value on the topic of trust itself. We all know that trust in business is important, especially when we want to become successful. We all know that trust is a critical factor; however, we often handle trust half-heartedly. We often treat people in any way we want, have no clear standards, and try to seek excuses with regard to trust.

There are many experts who claim to know how to become successful with trust, marketing and branding, but they treat the topic of trust as a goal only, rather than a legitimate part of branding success. How can that lead to success?

The reality is that trust is the first pillar of branding success. Trust is a topic to learn about. Many people know too little about trust. They have no basic background knowledge, they don't know how to build trust, they kill trust with false thinking and behaviour, and they're helpless when trust is broken.

There is so much false in our world with regard to trust. I have seen great problems with regard to trust, and I have therefore developed a new branding concept that encompasses the topics of trust, branding and entrepreneurship.

For me, branding is based on four pillars: 1. Trust, 2. Personality, 3. Leadership, 4. Brand.

You, as an entrepreneur, can only be successful in the long term, and have maximum success, when you learn about trust first. If you want to develop your full potential, you *must* learn about trust before you learn anything about branding. My new branding concept of becoming a Key Person of Trust sets new standards for branding.

How would it feel if you could overcome trust problems and become successful in branding? We would all love to be successful and convincing with our personality, leadership and brand. But how would it be to know that you are also successful with regard to trust?

Branding matters more than ever. In fact, it can be the key to your success. But trust matters, too, perhaps even more.

The Next Revolution in Branding: Becoming a Key Person of Trust, a powerhouse resource packed with inspiring and new insights, is based on new research. It outlines the four important pillars for becoming a Key Person of Trust (KPT): 1. Trust, 2. Personality, 3. Leadership, and 4. Brand. It provides an exclusive education for entrepreneurs who want to achieve more. It will change the way businesses approach trust, entrepreneurship and branding. It focuses on the things that really matter and that are necessary for having maximum and long-term success.

This book is a branding guide and workbook, invaluable for becoming a KPT and developing trust in business. It will allow you, the entrepreneur, to further develop your personality and leadership style, make a better impression, and become a trusted and respected brand. I will show you how to become a KPT so that you are best prepared for success.

Part I of the book covers every aspect of the topic of trust.

Part II discusses personality types, and gives inspiration and strategies for business success.

Part III deals with the 14 Key Components of Trust. These Key Components are influential in deciding when to give someone our trust. I explain their definition, their importance, and provide additional inspiration.

Part IV examines in detail the 10 Key Qualities of a KPT, and explains their importance and their role in achieving maximum success.

You can also profit from some BONUS MATERIAL and from VOICES OF EXPERTS (interviews of selected experts in different fields that contribute their special expertise and advice for being successful KPTs).

In this book, I cover in detail:

- How to have success with regard to trust
- Key Components for building trust
- What a KPT is and how you can become one
- Key Qualities of a KPT
- How to have maximum and long-term success as a KPT

Benefits of implementing what you learn in the book:

- Become successful with regard to trust
- Gain a new attitude with regard to success
- Gain self-trust and self-confidence
- Become authentic, credible and trustworthy
- Develop character and attitude
- Make a difference, become unique and distinctive
- Present better and perform better
- Become visible and attractive to contacts and dream customers
- Become a thought leader and build effective teams
- Convince with your own personal voice, message, mission and vision

- Create chances and opportunities, and get orders easily
- Develop a good reputation
- Enjoy more trust and influence

You will learn how to become a trustworthy leader and how to lead with trust. You will learn a new branding orientation. You will learn the skills to become successful, and the strategies to compete and stand out in the market.

With the help of this book, you can become a remarkable personality, a great leader, and a trusted and respected brand. The branding concept of KPT is your chance for success. With this book you will be prepared for success.

In every industry there are companies that are successful. They effortlessly attract loyal customers, create cool products or offer great services, and make lots of money. These are the companies that stand out.

Other companies have problems. The people work hard, make sacrifices, struggle, and dream of success, but their work does not pay off.

Most entrepreneurs have no real success, and part of the problem is that often they are blind optimists. They believe that entrepreneurship is about earning big money, making a big impact and living a life without worries. They follow the thinking: Work hard and be ambitious, and success will come.

This book will help those entrepreneurs, those who struggle to find a foothold in business. It will demystify the problem of how to find success in business. Success is no mystery. I will show you the way to success. By the end you'll know why you're not successful and what you should do to become successful.

The answers to these problems are often rooted in trust and branding. Entrepreneurs can be so focused on growing their business that they literally don't spend any time thinking about their personal brand.

I aim to help you find your way as an entrepreneur in the jungle of business relationships and business affairs. I will provide you with the necessary thinking, basis and inspiration to create your own brand with a new approach to trust.

With the help of this book you can become a KPT. To get the most from this book, follow these steps:

- Read carefully
- Figure out what the described problem is
- Write down your thoughts in a notebook
- Take short breaks between each chapter
- Talk about the content with others
- Think about your own situation
- Learn step by step
- Change your thinking
- Experiment with another attitude
- Practise what you have learned
- Don't blame yourself when things don't work
- Give yourself room to make mistakes
- Develop good habits
- Repeat what you have learned from time to time
- Don't try to be perfect

At the end of each chapter is a short takeaway that will give you a chance to reflect, rethink and learn.

When you reach the end of the book, read the advice of selected experts who have contributed their special expertise to the topic of becoming a successful KPT.

I will help you understand the topics of trust, branding and entrepreneurship, and explain what is important for your success. I will show you how to maximise your success.

Before you read any further, ask yourself: Who do I want to be in the future?

'It is never too late to be what you could have been.'

GEORGE ELIOT

PART I

TRUST AND ITS BACKGROUND

THE IMPORTANCE
OF TRUST

TRUST: A CRITICAL STRATEGIC ASSET

Before going any further in this book, there are a few points to understand:

1. Trustworthy behaviour is not about being perfect. There will always be good people who do unethical things. If a person isn't perfect, it doesn't mean they're in general bad. And there are certainly unethical people who try to find loopholes and rationalise their behaviour with their own orientation and attitude.
2. Trust must be personalised. It must have a human face and find a personal orientation if business leaders of today, and tomorrow, are to take them to heart.

3. And trust always permits new ideas. It would be false to insist too much on a certain strategy; a better way is to approach trust from a relaxed and open perspective.

If you want to be successful in business, you need to learn something about trust and its background, trustworthy leadership, and false thinking and behaviour.

Trust is a matter of mindset. Trust is not only a beneficial thing to have, but also a critical strategic asset in branding.

'Trust isn't a commodity that can be purchased. It is an asset that must be earned through transparency and truthfulness,' says Dion Chang, innovator, creative thinker, visionary and renowned trend analyst at Fluxtrends.

You can have the best marketing campaigns in the world, but if consumers don't trust you, either because you act unethically or you try to conceal the truth, they will switch to another brand.

The key for brands nowadays is trust. And it's not about people trusting other people. It's about people trusting a *brand*. We can put this in a formula:

$$BRAND + BEHAVIOUR = TRUST$$

And don't believe branding agencies that tell you that trust is not something you input to create an excellent brand. There are branding agencies that would have you believe that trust is only an outcome of an excellent brand. These agencies don't see trust as an element of a brand strategy. That is certainly false. Trust is a separate element in a branding concept.

If you want to be successful as a personality, leader and brand, you must do something for trust itself. You must learn something, and behave and act accordingly.

> *'The number one business rule*
> *reads: Trust begins with me.'*

KARIN SEBELIN

Summary

☑ Trust is a critical strategic asset when it comes to branding.

☑ Learning something about trust is important if you want to be successful in business.

THE IMPORTANCE
OF RELATIONSHIPS

RELATIONSHIPS ARE YOUR
SOCIAL CAPITAL

What is the most important asset in business? Your product, your service, your machines or your money? None of these. Your most important asset in business is the relationships you build. And by relationships I mean prospects, customers, suppliers and others in your supply chain.

You could come up with many reasons why this doesn't apply to you:

- I don't have the time to build relationships
- I don't know these people at all
- I want to protect my privacy

- I don't know whom to trust
- I have no passion for people

Many of these reasons are legitimate. But studies have shown how important it is to build relationships when it comes to business. And when I talk of relationships, I don't mean the sort of relationship that goes something like this: *Hi, you have a nice profile. Can I contact you?* Business relationships should be taken seriously and should be cared about.

It's not about intimacy. Effective relationships are about trust and understanding, and even empathy comes into play. Just trust plays a massive role in building business relationships, but it takes time to build trust and it can be destroyed in seconds.

Zig Ziglar, famous salesman and public speaker, summed it up well: 'If they like you, they will listen to you. If they trust you, they will do business with you.'

Without trust, business is not possible, although that doesn't mean that every relationship should be nurtured. It's sometimes better to be selective with regard to relationships and work with chosen people in a trustworthy way.

*'Business happens over years and years.
Value is measured in the total upside of
a business relationship, not by how much
you squeezed out in any one deal.'*

MARK CUBAN

Summary

☑ Relationships are your social capital and your most important asset in business.

☑ Without trust a successful business is not possible.

HOW TRUST IMPACTS YOUR LIFE

TRUST GETS IN THE WAY OF REALITY

Trust influences our relationships, family, partnerships, children, daily life and business life. Whenever we interact, we come into contact with trust. What is certainly clear is that trust impacts us three hundred and sixty-five days a year. It affects the quality of every relationship, every communication, and every effort in which we are engaged. Trust builds communities and leads to collaboration.

We tend to think about trust only in certain situations. For example if we lose a good friend or contact, we learn what trust means. Then suddenly we begin to appreciate people. When we want to build effective relationships, we must learn more about the topic of trust.

No matter what your relationships are, trust is always important. Trust is and will always be the foundation of life. Trust is part of your reality, and you're constantly coming into contact with it. You're often engaged with this topic, even when you're not aware.

Life happens, and you can't always influence the path it takes, just as you can't always influence your relationships. But you can convince with your personality, your character, your attitude and your presentation. All these things lead to trust.

Trust gives you the chance to be successful. All you need to do is seize that chance.

'Trust is the least understood, most neglected,
and most underestimated possibility of our time.'

STEPHEN COVEY

Summary

- ☑ Trust impacts every aspect of your life.
- ☑ You can impact your success through trust.

TRUST IS A SKILL
TO BE LEARNED

IN SCHOOL THERE ARE NO
LESSONS ON TRUST

We are not born knowing how to trust and so we need many teachers in life. Our parents teach us to trust. Life itself teaches us. Our experiences teach us. Few people receive a truly solid base of trust as children, and not every child is taught to trust itself. The problem is that in school there are no lessons on trust, so how can we really know how trust functions?

Trust is indeed a skill to be learned, and it is a choice to be made. Since we don't learn how to trust in school, we often have real problems as adults. We're insecure, and uncertain about how we will react when the right time for trust arrives.

Trust is a skill, and we should all learn that skill. Trust is based on the instinctive knowledge that no state is guaranteed forever. With regard to trust, in the end there is no real safety.

'All it takes is faith and trust.'

PETER PAN, PETER PAN

Summary

☑ Trust is a skill to be learned.

☑ You are not taught how to trust in school.

BEING TRUSTWORTHY IS NOT ALWAYS EASY

TRUSTWORTHINESS NEEDS DISCIPLINE

We live with a common truth: everything we say and do represents a choice, and how we decide determines and forms our lives. Making trustworthy decisions often requires our full attention and wisdom. It requires the ability to make distinctions between competing choices.

Through experience, we learn how to decide in the correct way. And it is good to know: being trustworthy is not always easy, but it is always important.

Trustworthiness needs discipline, and the will to make the right decision. In the end it is really about us. The real work comes from us. No one can simply read about trust and become trustworthy. It's not that easy.

Let's be clear: temptation is a constant; character is a choice. When we want to be successful discipline is the only way to go.

'Discipline is the bridge between
goals and accomplishment.'

JIM ROHN

Summary

☑ Trustworthiness is not always easy.

☑ Trustworthiness takes will and discipline.

6

THE IMPORTANCE OF TRUSTWORTHY LEADERSHIP

EACH PERSON HAS THEIR OWN PERSPECTIVE

What is meant by the term 'trustworthy leadership'? Whether you direct a small business, are in charge of a group in a larger organisation, or the head of a large agency, the issue of trustworthy leadership is one you cannot avoid. Ask a hundred people what they understand by the term 'trustworthy leadership' and you might get a hundred different answers.

Every one of us has a different understanding of trust and trustworthy leadership. Every individual person has their own perspective and defines what is right for them.

Trust is very important in life, especially if we want to be successful in business. In a business context, you can show your trust in many ways. The first step to becoming trustworthy is to take a look at your own behaviour before judging others. Knowing oneself—gaining self-awareness—is a primary quality of being viewed as trustworthy. Any leader will be more effective at leading outwardly if they first look within.

Soft skills, whether you win or lose people, are necessary for success. Your personal qualities are the key, and the first impression people have of you is an important step towards building relationships. Great leaders demonstrate that trust is an important company value. Great leaders are trust teachers.

Good communication within your company, and good interaction with team members and employees, is also very important. And customers must feel welcome, and that they have your support. As a business owner, you need to listen to what people have to say, demonstrate empathy and consideration, and be interested in their personal problems.

Be a trustworthy leader in communication. Demonstrate politeness and win hearts with sincere compliments and concern for the needs of others. A trustworthy leader must be a human leader. People will love you when they know you are here for them. A trustworthy leader *lives* trust, not just in business but also at home.

'Trust starts with trustworthy leadership. It must be built into the corporate culture.'

BARBARA BROOKS KIMMEL

Summary

☑ Everyone has their own understanding of trust, and trustworthy leadership.

☑ You have your own perspective, and define what is right for you.

☑ As a trustworthy leader, you will succeed through your personal qualities.

☑ A trustworthy leader is a human leader, and lives trust.

TRAITS OF TRUSTWORTHY LEADERS

TRUSTWORTHY LEADERS CONVINCE WITH THE RIGHT BEHAVIOUR

It is fair to say that trustworthy leaders have learned to act in the right way to create trust. Successful trustworthy leaders share many of the same traits:

- Honesty: they don't hide anything
- Reliability: they convince with integrity
- Dependability: they keep their promises and walk the walk
- Transparency: they admit their mistakes and problems
- Competency: they use their knowledge, intelligence, and expertise

- Benevolence: they are sympathetic and show good will
- Principled: they stand for what they believe in
- Grounding: they have a firm grasp of life and their future
- Control: they control their emotions and avoid overreacting
- Leadership: they lead with trust
- Fairness: they give other people a chance
- Helpfulness: they express encouragement towards others
- Trustworthiness: they practise open, trustworthy communication
- Understanding: they seek first to understand, and then to be understood
- Empathy: they have a real interest in other people, and their needs, interests and problems
- Win-win mindset: they know there is plenty for everyone and abundance is key
- Insight: they create synergies by seeing the potential in others' contributions

'Leadership should be born out of the understanding of the needs of those, who would be affected by it.'

MARIAN ANDERSON

Summary

☑ Your behaviour is critical when it comes to achieving success.

☑ You need to monitor your behaviour to become a trustworthy leader.

BECOME A TRUSTWORTHY LEADER

LEADERS DON'T BECOME TRUSTWORTHY BY ACCIDENT

To become a trustworthy leader, you need a clear understanding of what trust means for you personally and a strong willingness to develop your own personality further.

You may already practise trustworthy leadership to a greater or lesser extent. Regardless, your understanding should align with that of the framework, mission and vision of the organisation you are a part of.

Trust should be talked about, always, but more importantly, trust is about acting, too. When practised correctly, a trustworthy leadership builds trust, and brings credibility and respect, both for you and the organisation. It leads to a good reputation. Trust builds your brand.

Another positive outcome of a trustworthy leadership is good collaboration and the creation of a healthy climate within your company. A trustworthy leadership is simply the right way to go.

'When consumers purchase a Toyota, they are not simply purchasing a car, truck or van. They are placing their trust in our company.'

AKIO TOYODA

Summary

☑ Leaders don't become trustworthy by accident. They learn the behaviours of trust, and practise them over a period of time to the point where they become habits.

☑ Learn to practise trustworthy leadership.

☑ Trust is not just about talking, but acting, too.

☑ Trust builds your brand.

TRUST AND CULTURAL BARRIERS

WHAT CULTURE ARE YOU A PART OF?

We might assume that if every culture practised the same kind of thinking life would be easy; there would be fewer problems with trust. Trust is lived and practised differently in different countries, and no single standard of trust exists for all people. Thus, no one has the right to criticise other cultures that have a different approach to trust. Unfortunately, being in one culture can mean intolerance of other cultures. Cultural norms vary from people to people, and there will always be intolerance.

What kind of culture are you a part of? Think about where you fit in in the following areas:

- Race and ethnicity
- Gender
- Family heritage
- Sexual orientation
- Place of residence
- Main passions in life
- Career or place of work
- Hobbies
- Religion

Finding your place among these different categories should give you a clue about the problems that can arise with regard to trust. When you deal with people from other countries, you would do well to find out what is their default understanding of trust.

In China, for example, the default setting is toward distrust. People in China build trust first, and when that is achieved, they do business. For them, it is about developing *guanxi first*. The Chinese term *guanxi* is used to describe relationships that are mutually beneficial.

In Western society, the default setting is toward trust. People are generally seen as trustworthy, until they do something that breaks that trust.

There exist two forms of trust: cognitive and affective. Cognitive trust comes from the head. It is based on the confidence that the other person is reliable, has skills and will accomplish something. Affective trust comes from the heart. It is based on feelings of emotional closeness, friendship and empathy.

What about you? Do you trust with your head or with your heart?

There are cultures that are more task-based. Here business people are more likely to develop connections based largely on cognitive trust. Examples of such countries are Germany, Denmark, the United States, the UK and Australia.

Other cultures are more relationship-based, and trust is built by developing personal bonds. Examples of such countries are China, Brazil and Saudi Arabia. When it comes to business in these cultures, cognitive and affective trust are not separate issues but instead are woven together.

Learn to have an understanding of other cultures. Learn to be interested in their history, lives and traditions. Learn the different aspects of their lives that differentiate them from your own culture. Being open to the differences in other cultures will lead to trust.

'One of the most effective ways to learn about oneself is by taking seriously the cultures of others. It forces you to pay attention to those details of life, which differentiate them from you.'

EDWARD T HALL, THE SILENT LANGUAGE

Summary

☑ All human beings, regardless of their cultural background, have a strong desire to develop relationships, and trust is crucial in this process.

☑ Prejudice against other cultures with regard to trust is not the way to success.

☑ Being open and interested in other cultures will lead to trust.

☑ There exist two forms of trust with regard to culture: cognitive and affective trust.

10

TRUST IS A COMPLEX THING

THERE ARE MANY DEFINITIONS OF TRUST

So far we have learned two things: trust plays a great role in business and in life, and much stands and falls because of trust. Now we'll define the word *trust*. What is trust? This is not an easy question to answer. The *Oxford English Dictionary* defines the word *trust* as 'firm belief in the reliability, truth, or ability of someone or something'.

'Trust is complex,' says Tim Caulfield of the University of Alberta.

'There is a large literature base on trust in different disciplines, and the definitions are 'somewhat abstract,' says Cary Funk of the Pew Research Center.

Key words in the definition of trust include *benefits*, *risks*, *uncertainty*, *credibility* and *vulnerability*.

This interesting definition of trust by science blogger, Liz Neeley, combines multiple academic definitions of trust: 'Your willingness to embrace the advice of a group of strangers, because you believe they (a) know the truth, (b) will tell you the truth as they know it; and (c) have your best interest at heart, all of which depend on (d) who you are, (e) who they are, and (f) what you're talking about.'

I especially like this definition by James Grunig, University of Maryland: 'The willingness to open oneself to risk by engaging in a relationship with another party.' He emphasises that a person's 'openness to risk is the important element' of trust. According to Grunig, trust has three dimensions:

1. Integrity: the belief that a person or organisation is fair and just
2. Dependability: the belief that a person or organisation will do what they say
3. Confidence: the belief that a person or organisation has the ability to do what they say they will do

Cynthia Lynn Wall (LCSW) in her book, *The Courage to Trust: A Guide to Building Deep and Lasting Relationships*, also speaks of three things:

1. Trust is a feeling.
2. Trust is a choice.
3. Trust is a skill that can be learned.

And now for my own explanation of what trust is.

Trust is the expectation by a person, group, or company that another person, group or company will act in an ethically justifiable manner; the expectation of morally correct decisions and actions based on ethical principles.

Trust requires goodwill. It is associated with loyalty and resiliency. It is an invaluable organisational asset. It impacts the quality of every business relationship, and has a positive influence on the growth of a company.

In any organisation, people should communicate openly and honestly. Good business should be conducted with competence, fairness, integrity, transparency and authenticity. It is about reliability and is led by moral and ethical standards.

Also central to the idea of trust are empathy, compassion and benevolence, and the expectation that people within an organisation demonstrate good motives and intentions. Trust is the glue of business and social exchange. Trust creates more trust. It is generative. The more signals of trust we share, the more trust increases.

However, trust can't be forced. Conditions must be created whereby people give their trust freely. When people choose to trust, effective cooperation and collaboration between people is possible.

Trust is a delicate thing and lies in the eye of the beholder. What does that mean? It means that our behaviour can destroy the trust around us without our being aware. We might assume having a fine behaviour, but others could feel annoyed or even scared off.

Trust always involves a risk: the risk of being hurt or disappointed. It includes vulnerability, and the possibility that another person will act opportunistically or in a self-serving manner.

Some people may claim that trust has to develop over time, but that is a false belief. We should give our trust and express our confidence in people immediately to receive their trust in return. Trust does not mean security, but it does offer the chance of interesting and effective relationships between human beings.

How do you personally define trust? How does your business define trust? How does your business measure trust? Is your definition of trust the same as your customers' and suppliers'?

'... trust is a term with many meanings.'

WILLIAMSON 1993: 453

Summary

☑ Trust means different things to different people.

☑ Trust is a complex thing; it lies in the eye of the beholder.

A FEW FACTS
ABOUT TRUST

WHAT YOU SHOULD KNOW
ABOUT TRUST

Beyond trust in personal relationships, too often we don't have a clear picture of what trust really means. Here some facts about trust:

- Fact 1: We know much better what trust does than what trust is. Equally, everyone has their own understanding of trust, and most of us understand what trust does much better than we understand what trust is. Some people have problems with trust and don't know how to solve those problems.
- Fact 2: We could not exist without trust. Families depend on it, and marriages are built on it. Any kind of partnership requires it, whether it's a business or personal partnership. It's no different

at work and in business. Trust increases engagement and productivity, and fosters good communication. It leads to good relationships and is the driving force for success. Trust is the glue, the lubricant and the oxygen of business and social exchange. And without basic trust—trust in our world, in our technology, in our societies, and in mankind in general—we would be lost. We simply must trust if we want to be successful.

- Fact 3: Trust has something to do with our belief systems. We could say trust is a belief about the goodness or rationality of others.
- Fact 4: Trust is too often taken for granted, misunderstood, and even severely underestimated. We think we have people's trust and then suddenly wake up and realise that we do not. A French proverb says: 'Fish discover water last.' In other words, fish are unaware of the existence of the water until the water level drops too low or the water becomes polluted. In the same way, people discover trust last. Too often we take trust for granted until we lose people's trust.
- Fact 5: Trust is a task that needs care. Trust is something we face every day and there is much to learn about it. It does not work like that: 'I will learn a new thinking!' and the next day we forget everything again.
- Fact 6: Trust is no half-hearted concept. A trustworthy leadership is not about reading a book, or learning something by heart and then practising it full of optimism, word by word, without any mistakes and to perfection. Trust is no mayfly that lives for a day and then dies. Trust is a concept that needs will and commitment. Doing things half-heartedly never makes sense. Trust is too important to be dealt with half-heartedly.

- Fact 7: Trust is not a relationship; it is a quality in you. Trust is a key leadership quality. Not everyone is able to lead with trust. Roman and Greek philosophers agreed that a leader should be temperate, self-controlled, respectable, hospitable, able to teach, nonviolent and gentle, and sincere. A leader is an example or model of desired behaviour that is able to pass on these qualities to others.
- Fact 8: Trust is a virtue, which means having faith and confidence in others.
- Fact 9: Trust involves a risk and will always be insecure. We never know how a story ends. Does a person betray us? Does the person cheat? Does the person act opportunistically or in a self-serving manner? Even with cooperation, confidence and faith, there exists a freedom to disappoint another's expectations.
- Fact 10: Trust offers chances. Trust can boost our chances of business success. *Know me, like me, trust me*: this is the principle that creates valuable relationships. People know and learn to like us before they trust us.

Becoming a Key Person of Trust (KPT) in business is a great chance. Everything is possible when you behave and act in the right way. When you show that you are authentic, credible and honest, and that you do a great job as a respected expert in your field, people will like you and trust you more easily.

'Facts are many, but the truth is one.'

RABINDRANATH TAGORE

Summary

☑ Trust is a complex topic, and it can be difficult to understand what it really means.

☑ Learning some facts about trust is necessary.

TRUST SHOWS YOUR HUMANITY

TRUST HAS A HUMAN FACE

Trust is something personal. We are masters at categorising, and we'll often try to use one kind of trust in our professional lives and another in our private lives at home. This can become confusing and often creates complications.

How do you deal with trust?

Decide which of these answers best applies to you:

- I have a different standard of trust in business.
- I have no special standard of trust in business.
- Trust is trust to me, no matter where I am.

Why do we make these differentiations with regard to trust?

Trust shows our humanity, our good character, and our personality.

'Corporations are collections of people, and we ought to insist that those people (that would be us) do the right thing. Business is too powerful for us to leave our humanity at the door of the office. It's not business, it's personal.'

SETH GODIN

☑ Trust is something personal.

☑ Trust has a human face.

Summary ☑ Trust shows your humanity.

INCREASE TRUST THROUGH BEHAVIOUR

EVERY INTERACTION IS A MOMENT OF TRUST

Behaviour matters, especially when it comes to building trust. In every one of your relationships, what you do and how you do it has a greater impact than anything you say. You can tell someone that you love them, but only through the right actions can you convince them of this. Words can be wonderful, but without the right actions they are useless. Words need to be followed by the right validating behaviour to increase trust. Remember, each interaction with another person is a moment of trust. Hank Paulson of Goldman Sachs said: 'Trust is established through action.'

Some suggestions for increasing trust through behaviour:

- Talk straight and tell the truth
- Show respect, kindness and consideration
- See people as individuals
- Show appreciation
- Create transparency
- Know what's right and what's wrong
- Show loyalty and give credit to others
- Deliver results
- Improve your abilities
- Confront reality
- Clarify expectations and make things happen
- Practise accountability
- Extend trust; trust people and they will trust you
- Listen first before you speak and act, without judgement and by engaging in real dialogue
- Keep your commitments; do what you say you will do
- Let other people become involved in the decision-making process
- Offer positive feedback
- Be responsive, and answer messages
- Be supportive and willing to help others
- Give more than you take

*'The ABCs are attitude, behaviour
and communication skills.'*

GERALD CHERTAVIAN

Summary

☑ Keep in mind that each interaction with another person is a moment of trust.

☑ Learn to increase trust through your behaviour.

THE ROLE OF TRUST IN BUSINESS

TRUST IS THE DRIVER THAT FUELS BUSINESSES

Our world today is getting more and more complex and impersonal. Not that long ago, we knew the people and businesses with which we interacted, and exchanged money and services. Now, as more and more commerce is conducted online, you're more likely to order your goods and services via your smartphone or your computer. This increasingly impersonal nature of our dealings with other people requires a great deal of trust.

Trust is at the heart of our daily interactions. It is the driver that fuels business. Trust fosters productivity. The good thing about trust is that you can't fake it. And when people fake trust we often recognise it. Trust means caring about the other person or people.

And actions speak louder than words. In fact, action is the best way to show trust.

In business, there are many important points to keep in mind:

- Know yourself and know how to interpret things
- Tell the truth
- Recognise other people's perspectives
- Encourage others to speak the truth
- Practise having unpleasant conversations (life is not about steadily saying YES)
- Admit your mistakes (so that others learn to admit them, too)
- Build transparency
- Trust your employees to do the right thing

In the past, trust was built by close proximity, but now businesses must cultivate it in other ways. How to build trust today:

- Provide quality products and services
- Provide reliable and excellent customer support
- Offer secure shopping experiences, for example, SSL (secure sockets layer) protocol on website
- Have a professional website
- Include testimonials and reviews on your website
- Share positive media and PR stories
- Share information transparently (being honest and open with your clients and prospects)
- etc.

What about you? What is the current level of trust within your company? What could you do to help increase it?

'Trust is the lubrication that makes it possible for organisations to work.'

WARREN BENNIS

Summary

☑ Trust is of the utmost importance in business.

☑ Trust fuels businesses and fosters productivity.

☑ Establishing trust within your company and among your clients is imperative to achieving success regardless of your industry.

COMMON MISCONCEPTIONS ABOUT TRUST

RIGID THINKING HINDERS SUCCESS

Trust is a nebulous topic and everyone has a different understanding of what the word means. The following trust myths exist in our society, and it is worth taking a closer look at them:

- *Trust is built solely on integrity:* No, trust is a function of character (which includes integrity) and competence.
- *You either have trust or you don't:* Trust can be created, and it can also be destroyed.
- *Trust is all or nothing:* There are people who believe that trusting means trusting in *all* things, but trusting someone

for one thing does not necessarily mean trusting them for everything.

- *Lost trust cannot be restored:* It is certainly not easy to 'heal' broken trust, but most of the time lost trust can be restored.
- *Trust cannot be taught:* Trust can indeed be taught and learned, and can be used to advantage.
- *There is too much risk in trusting people*: Not trusting people is the greater risk.
- *Trust must be earned:* We should not concentrate too much on this old-school thinking. The business rule no. 1 reads: 'Trust begins with me.' — Karin Sebelin. We should give our trust first so others learn to trust us, too. When we concentrate too much on trustworthiness, we risk developing ambitiousness, hypocrisy and false behaviour. In the end, we become 'trust hunters'. Permanent concentration on trustworthiness may lead to negative behaviour.

*'Trust means forgetting all the
trust myths that exist.'*

KARIN SEBELIN

Summary

☑ Forget all those myths about trust; they will only hinder your success.

ADOPT ANOTHER MINDSET

CHANGE YOUR THINKING

It's time to change your thinking and begin to see trust with new eyes. To trust is a self-empowered choice. Trust starts with you; you can control what you do. If you choose to trust a person you will find your own reasons for that trust. And if you choose not to trust, you will keep your distance. Trust is a personal choice.

Trust is an inside job: you choose how you want to feel. Choose to trust, if that's what your heart desires. If you want to trust, you can. Choose how you want to feel and start creating those feelings now. Be present, and make a soul-centred choice. Choose your thoughts and actions wisely.

Stop focusing on other people's faults. Rather than making others responsible for the way you feel, concentrate on yourself and you will live a happier life. Life is not about steadily blaming others. You should give other people a fair chance.

It is not about: *If you behave, then I will trust you.* Forget any if-this-then-that thinking. It kills relationships and puts conditions on love. You should give unconditional love.

Change your thinking and change your culture. See trust with new eyes.

> '*The world, as we have created it, is a process of our thinking. It cannot be changed without changing our thinking.*'

ALBERT EINSTEIN

Summary

☑ In order to be successful you may need to change how you think about trust.

☑ Learn to adopt another trust culture.

TRUST-KILLING BEHAVIOURS

TRUST CAN BE EASILY WEAKENED AND LOST

It is very easy to torpedo trust, often inadvertently, and often during situations where there is heightened pressure or visibility. Trust is created over time through consistent actions, but it can be weakened and lost quickly. A leader must always be conscious of their behaviour. Here some trust-killing behaviours that leaders should avoid:

- Criticising others in public: Public criticism is bad behaviour and will make people look small-minded. Steadily pointing out mistakes and criticising others in public destroys trust.

- Overreacting to mistakes: Trust is killed if a leader overreacts when mistakes are made. Avoid saying things like, 'Not again.'
- Keeping someone under constant surveillance: Constantly checking someone's work will make them feel undervalued and underestimated, leading to a loss of trust.
- Withholding information: A leader who withholds important information that someone else needs to complete their job is showing lack of trust.
- Lying, or telling alternative stories: Outright lying, or telling a different story undercuts trust.
- Excluding people from the inner circle: Publicly excluding someone from the inner circle does not foster trust.
- Not being transparent: Transparency is an important element in business. Good leaders are transparent and don't hide anything.
- Taking credit for others' ideas: Giving credit to those who deserve it is very important in business. When a leader takes credit for other people's ideas and results it kills trust.
- Not walking the walk: When a leader says one thing but acts in another way entirely, without explanation, they appear untrustworthy. You should walk the walk, which means doing what you say you will do.
- Dictating what others should do: Rather than being dictatorial, a good leader will ask for input on an assignment. When influence is denied, trust is eroded.

'Trust is hard to earn and quickly destroyed.'

KARIN SEBELIN

Summary

☑ As a leader, you must remain conscious of your behaviour at all times.

☑ Trust can be quickly destroyed.

☑ Make every attempt not to behave in a trust-killing way.

PART II

TRUST AND PERSONALITY TYPES

HUMAN BEHAVIOUR: FOUR PERSONALITY TYPES

RELATING TO PEOPLE IS NOT ALWAYS EASY

It is important to understand the different personality types if you want to be successful. No two humans are exactly alike. That is one reason why many of us have problems with their relationships. Each of us has a different worldview, belief system, and a different consciousness.

There is a way that you can communicate with the people in your life so that you feel heard, understood, appreciated and taken seriously. A study on human behaviour[1] has revealed that ninety

---

1   This study was published in the journal Science Advances by researchers from Universidad Carlos III de Madrid, together with colleagues from the universities of

percent of us can be classified into four basic personality types with regard to human behaviour:

1. Optimistic: People who believe that they and their partner will make the best choice for both of them (20 percent of the results).
2. Pessimistic: They select the option they see as the lesser of two evils (also 20 percent of the results).
3. Trusting: Born collaborators who always cooperate, no matter whether they win or lose (also 20 percent of the results).
4. Envious: The most common type (30 percent compared to 20 percent for the other groups).

Now you could certainly ask if it matters whether or not you know other people's personalities? I think it does matter, because each of us has a zone of comfort, and a zone of ability. By knowing our areas of comfort and challenge we are able to guide ourselves. By understanding other people's personality types we can better relate to them.

'Our personalities define our realities.'

WAYNE GERARD TROTMAN

Barcelona, Rovira I Virgili and Zaragoza. The study analysed the responses of 541 volunteers.

Summary

☑ Understand the four different personality types with regard to human behaviour so you relate to other people in a better way.

SELLING: FOUR PERSONALITY TYPES

LEARN HOW TO SELL EFFECTIVELY

If you want to constantly win deals and become successful in selling, you can't sell the way you would like to be sold to. You have to adapt your strategy to the buyer's personality. And this is where it's important to learn something about the different types of personalities, too. Keep in mind that your prospective buyer can be a mix of all four personality types rather than fitting neatly into one category.

In the context of selling, there are four main types of personalities:

1. Assertive: They tend to use declarative sentences and ask few questions. They speak a little louder than average, and use confident and animated body language. How to sell to this type:
    - Be professional.
    - Get to the point quickly and don't waste their time.
    - Emphasise how your product will solve their problems.

2. Amiable: They value personal relationships, and want to trust their business partners. They like new challenges, which means they will dive enthusiastically into finding creative solutions. They don't make decisions quickly, so you should expect a longer sales process than usual. As they are great listeners, they might take an interest in you and ask personal questions. They will be friendly, calm and patient during meetings. How to sell to this type:
    - Take on the role of an expert and act as an advisor.
    - Give them personal guarantees since they are more risk averse than other types.
    - Bring up examples of similar clients and cases that have been successful for you.
    - Paint a vision and help them visualise the outcome.

3. Expressive: They are sometimes called humanists, and with good reason: they value their personal relationships. They are much concerned with others' wellbeing. They care. They are enthusiastic, creative, spontaneous, outgoing and rely on their intuition. They put much weight on respect, friendship and loyalty. How to sell to this type:
    - Emphasise the relationship and offer exceptional customer service.
    - Avoid concentrating too much on data, facts and figures.
    - Present case studies.
    - Summarise what there is to learn.

4. Analytic: They love facts, figures and data, and want to get to the facts quickly. They stick to their deadlines. They do not make decisions quickly, preferring to understand the details and options available to them before making any decision. They are more logical and cautious than any other personality type, and in conversations they are direct, formal and serious. They won't spend time getting to know you on a personal level. How to sell to this type:

- Don't try to force the relationship.
- Never rush; give them time and be prepared for a longer sales process.
- They will have done some research, which means you can spend less time outlining basic features.
- Don't overhype your product; this will only make them suspicious.
- Offer as much detailed information as possible.

> *'Sales are contingent upon the attitude of the salesman, not the attitude of the prospect.'*
>
> **W CLEMENT STONE**

Summary

☑ You need to understand the four personality types in order to sell effectively.

☑ Learn how each personality type behaves and reacts, and adapt your behaviour accordingly.

PERSONALITY-BASED MARKETING: THE BIG FIVE PERSONALITY TRAITS

KNOW HOW TO CONNECT WITH OTHERS

Marketing nowadays is all about psychology, and knowing how to connect with others. To succeed in marketing, you will need to know something about personality-based marketing. This type of marketing can create a better match for products, services or experiences, and makes it possible for you to reach people by their personality type and how they see the world. Personality-based marketing allows you to communicate and engage with others in a more effective way.

In this context, personality can be defined as individual differences of thinking, feeling and behaving. After studying millions of personality profiles, psychologists have concluded that the unlimited number of different personality descriptions can be reduced to five basic factors. These personality factors are called 'The Big Five Personality Traits'. Learn them here:

1. O = Openness to experience
   Low = conventional, traditional
   High = curious, adventurous
   Personality facets: adventurousness, artistic interests, emotionality, imagination, intellect, liberalism
2. C = Conscientiousness
   Low = impulsive, disorganised
   High = self-disciplined, methodical
   Personality facets: achievement striving, cautiousness, dutifulness, orderliness, self-discipline, self-efficacy
3. E = Extraversion
   Low = quiet, reserved
   High = social, gregarious
   Personality facets: high activity level, assertiveness, cheerfulness, excitement seeking, friendliness, gregariousness
4. A = Agreeableness
   Low = sceptical, self-interested
   High = trusting, group-oriented
   Personality facets: altruism, cooperation, modesty, morality, sympathy, trust
5. N = Neuroticism (also called emotional stability)
   Low = calm, unflappable
   High = worries more, easily made anxious

Personality facets: anger, anxiety, depression, immoderation, self-consciousness, vulnerability

Use personality-based marketing and learn to match the tone and framing of your communication of marketing with the personality profiles and thinking styles of your potential customers, and you will boost your effectiveness. If you know a person's personality style, you can customise how you engage them.

> *'Marketing is a contest for people's attention.'*
>
> **SETH GODIN**

Summary

☑ Learn the Big Five Personality Traits to better communicate and engage with others.

☑ Use personality-based marketing to craft your message, advertising or content to match the different personality types, while also considering the stage of the customer journey at which you plan to engage.

PART III

KEY COMPONENTS FOR BUILDING TRUST

KEY COMPONENT 1: BASIC TRUST

THE FOUNDATION OF LIFE

We have discussed trust and the right attitude to promote trust and success, and learned something about different personality types. Now it's time to dive into the first of the 14 Key Components for building trust, the first of which is basic trust.

We often act from a position of basic trust when we give others our trust. Basic trust is essential for a happy life. The term 'basic trust' results from psychology, or sociology. Basic trust is the precondition that allows you to go into the unknown, and accept not knowing. Basic trust means that you have a good feeling about your life, and that it is unfolding and evolving in the right way.

You need basic trust in your daily life and to know that everything will work well. The water will come out of the pipe, the supermarket will be filled with goods, and the traffic will flow.

A well-developed sense of basic trust is a great and important gift parents can give to a child. Basic trust, or the confidence that life and people are good, develops in the first years of the life of a child. It helps to form the character of the child, and later of the adult. Basic trust is the basis of healthy self-trust, a positive attitude to life, and a happy life.

Strong basic trust is the foundation every person needs before they can trust in other things:

- Themselves and their own skills
- Development of self-esteem
- Ability to love
- Bonds with other people: friendship and relationships of love
- Knowledge that life in general is basically good

How does basic trust develop? A newborn has few basic needs: food, warmth, security and care. When an infant has a need, it cries. Its parents just have to find out what the problem is. Basic trust is built when parents care reliably for their child, when they recognise a need and satisfy it. The child learns: *My parents care for me when I need something. I feel comfortable and cared for. When* loving care is added, and frequent body and skin contact, the child develops the feeling of being loved.

If certain circumstances should intervene, for example if the child is separated from its parents, is neglected or treated badly, then it could develop a deep distrust towards other people. The result is pessimism, lack of attachment, or even mental disorder and depression.

We can say, therefore, that basic trust is learned behaviour that can date back to childhood.

'Learning to trust is one of life's most difficult tasks.'

ISAAC WATTS

Summary

☑ Basic trust is the 1st Key Component of the trust-building process.

☑ We often act out of basic trust when we give others our trust.

☑ Basic trust is the basis of a good life.

☑ Trust develops in a favourable environment and with a stable constellation of people surrounding a child, especially in the presence of caring parents.

☑ Basic trust represents the cornerstone of a healthy personality.

KEY COMPONENT 2: NEEDS

LIVING A HEALTHY AND SUCCESSFUL LIFE

Needs refer to everything necessary to live a healthy and successful life. We all have needs, and these needs drive us as human beings. We often act out of needs when we give others our trust.

What are needs? *The Oxford English Dictionary* definition of need: 'A requirement, a thing wanted, circumstances requiring some course of action.'

Needs can be defined by three criteria:

- Universal (they are all relevant to human beings)
- Contextual (they depend on the context, the situation and the circumstance)

- Personal (we all define needs differently according to our experiences and beliefs)

Needs underpin our thoughts, feelings and behaviour. They fuel the urges inside us that cause us to act. Maslow's hierarchy of needs (1943) is a motivational theory in psychology, a model of human needs. American psychologist Abraham Maslow stated that people are motivated to achieve certain needs and that some of these needs take precedence over others. The different needs according to Maslow's hierarchy of needs (see the model):

- Physiological needs: The basic need in this hierarchy is the need for physical survival (food, water, warmth, rest), and it is the first thing that motivates our behaviour. If such needs, like food, are not satisfied, the body cannot function optimally.
- Need for safety: The next level, after the first has been fulfilled, is the need for safety (for security).

  Physiological needs and the need for safety are both basic needs, and important to the physical survival of the person. When individuals have basic nutrition, shelter and safety they will attempt to accomplish more.
- Need for love and belonging: This includes intimate relationships with friends and family, being part of a group.
- Need for esteem: Maslow divided this need (prestige and feeling of accomplishment) into two sub-categories: 1) esteem for oneself; dignity, achievement, and 2) the desire for a good reputation and respect from others; status, prestige.

  The need for love and belonging, and the need for esteem are both psychological needs. Maslow considered physiological needs the most important.

- Need for self-actualisation: This is when someone achieves their full potential, which can include creative activities and personal growth. Maslow described it as 'a desire 'to become everything one is capable of becoming'.
This need is a self-fulfilment need.

This model with its five different needs can be divided into deficiency needs and growth needs. The first four needs cover deficiency, and the last is considered a growth need.

What do these terms mean? Deficiency needs motivate people when, for instance, those needs are unmet. For example, if we go without food for a long time there will be consequences: we will get hungry.

Growth needs are there for personal development. Whether these needs are harmful or beneficial depends on how they are satisfied, by our parents when we are young, and by other people when we are mature.

Unsatisfied needs can lead to neuroses, pathologies and depression, and we can become ill. Our values, thoughts, emotions and actions are all initially formed to satisfy those most basic needs.

Pyramid showing Maslow's hierarchy of needs:[2]

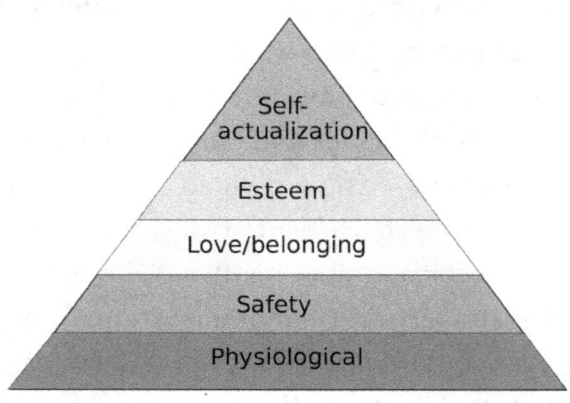

---

2 Wikimedia, author FireflySixtySeven.

*'We all have different desires and needs,
but if we don't discover, what we want
from ourselves and what we stand for, we
will live passively and unfulfilled.'*

BILL WATTERSON

Summary

☑ Needs are the 2nd Key Component of the trust-building process.

☑ We often act out of needs when we give others our trust.

☑ We all have needs that we want to be fulfilled.

☑ Some needs are necessary for survival; others are useful for personal success.

☑ Having your needs met builds trust.

KEY COMPONENT 3: WISHES

OUR DESIRES IN LIFE

We often act out of wishes when we give others our trust. We all have desires in life. That is only normal. What are wishes? Wishes are our desires, our longings. What wishes do you have? Do you wish to be successful? Do you wish to build better relationships?

Times have changed. In our modern times, it is mostly about having the newest technology, the newest smartphone. We are focused on technology. We want the newest things. We have not yet learned that less is more. A constant focus on possessing everything is not the perfect way to go.

With the growth of the internet and online commerce, we often forget our humanity. We overlook that life is about relationships, interesting connections, and trust. And when we are not successful, we wonder where the problem is. The problem is within us.

Too often we do not have the right feeling for trust. We wish we had more contacts instead of getting to know people better. We wish we had more influence instead of learning that success is about trust. We wish we were more successful instead of doing something for trust. You see where the problem is? We want too much and learn too little.

'Some people want it to happen, some wish it would happen, others make it happen.'

MICHAEL JORDAN

Summary

☑ Wishes are the 3rd Key Component of the trust-building process.

☑ We often act out of wishes when we give others our trust.

☑ Wishes are not necessarily bad, but you should have the right ones.

24

KEY COMPONENT 4: EXPECTATIONS

EXPECTATIONS CAN LEAD TO DISAPPOINTMENT

What do you expect from life? What do you expect from others? We all have certain expectations in life. What are expectations? The *Oxford English Dictionary* defines an expectation as 'an act or instance of expecting or looking forward, thing expected or hoped for, probability of an event'.

An expectation is a strong belief that something will happen, or that someone will do something. If we apply that to our relationships, it sets us up for failure. Of course, we all have expectations in life. That is normal.

We often act out of expectations when we give others our trust. Every time we enter into a new relationship, or have an interaction with another person, company or product, we have certain expectations. Sometimes we are aware of these expectations and sometimes not. Many people's expectations are too high, and they have too many of them. And when their expectations aren't met they are disappointed or angry.

Osho said: 'People expect too much. And if our expectations are not fulfilled, then we feel frustrated. Then we feel constantly, as if we propose and God goes on disposing; we feel that God is the enemy; we feel as if everybody is against us and everybody is working against us.'

Many of us expect other people to behave in the way we want, and to give us their attention. Or we expect to be successful in scores, rankings and competitions. We expect life to be our servant, and when things go against our understanding we become frustrated.

It would be far better if we learned to have a genuine interest in other people; if we learned to care about other people and demonstrated through our actions how much we care; and if we learned to support other people without expecting anything in return.

Where do our expectations come from? Often from our own experiences with another person, or from similar experiences that other people have had. They come from what we read, hear or see, as well as from what others tell us.

How often have you been disappointed when someone failed to support you in the way you wanted? Why is it important for you to pay attention to those missed expectations? When expectations are met people work well together and trusting relationships flourish. When they are not met, however, things become harder. People struggle and relationships suffer.

*'I believe expectations are
premeditated resentment.'*

RUDY RASMUS

Summary

☑ Expectations are the 4th Key Component of the trust-building process.

☑ We often act out of expectations when we give others our trust.

☑ Too many or too high expectations are not the way to success.

☑ You should reduce your expectations when you interact with other people.

25

KEY COMPONENT 5: HABITS

CHANGE YOUR HABITS, CHANGE YOUR LIFE

If you want to be successful, start changing your habits. It is never too late to change your habits. What are habits? According to Wikipedia, 'Habits are routines of behaviour that are repeated regularly and tend to occur subconsciously.'

Habits are actions performed with little conscious thought and often unwittingly triggered by external cues. They influence our behaviour and can be our greatest allies for positive change. They are often difficult to break, and are also frequent saboteurs of personal progress and success. Gretchen Rubin, author of the book *Better Than Before: Mastering the Habit of Our Everyday Lives*, summed it up so well: 'Habit is a good servant, but a bad master.'

What habits do you have? Ever thought about your habits? Do you know that your habits are critical for relationships? We often act out of habits when we give others our trust. Knowing your own habits exactly is essential to creating habits for success. Knowing yourself and what motivates you to take action is the key to creating the life you want.

Whether your habits are focused on business, writing, relationships or other things, excellence and success are just the result of your deeply ingrained habits. Understanding the psychology of habits can help you change them. Creating new and the right habits is one of the hardest things to do, but it's essential when you want to become successful in life.

What is important for you in life? Money? Wealth? Relationships? Be honest.

Aristotle said, 'We are what we repeatedly do. Excellence then, is not an act, but a habit.' We can influence our lives and determine what is important for us. We are the masters of our own luck.

'Your beliefs become your thoughts,
Your thoughts become your words,
Your words become your actions,
Your actions become your habits,
Your habits become your values,
Your values become your destiny.'

MAHATMA GANDHI

Summary

☑ Habits are the 5th Key Component of the trust-building process.

☑ We often act out of habits when we give others our trust.

☑ Know yourself, and influence your life and habits positively.

☑ Influence your relationships positively.

26

KEY COMPONENT 6: PRINCIPLES

THE LIFE WE IMAGINE

What kind of principles do you have? What are your guiding principles? Each person has certain principles. That is normal. We often act out of principles when we give others our trust. What are principles? Principles are beliefs that are learned and adopted over time, during our lives. Principles are our imagination of life, the way we see the world and how the world works for us. Principles are our guidelines for human behaviour.

Ever heard the term 'person of principles'? This is meant as a compliment. Such a person faithfully follows a principle or set of principles rather than abandoning them when they become inconvenient. If faced with a difficult decision in life, a person of principle will refer to their guiding set of principles. Such people are generally highly moral and make excellent ethical choices.

Having principles is very important nowadays for business success. Learn to be a person of principles. Defining your beliefs and guiding principles is important in the running of a successful business. If you don't define your principles and beliefs, others— friends, associates or the marketplace—will do it for you.

It is also advisable to set clear boundaries in life. Learn to say no from time to time. Boundaries are liberating. Time, for example, is a valuable resource, and time is often limited. Being selective with your time will ensure that you have enough time for yourself and your family. If you don't set clear boundaries in your life, you risk ending up imprisoned by the limits others have set for you. Until people in the modern world have learned to respect our life a bit more, these boundaries are a good way to escape the pressure they put on us.

'Principles are guidelines for human conduct that are proven to have enduring, permanent value.'

STEPHEN R COVEY

Summary

☑ Principles are the 6th Key Component of the trust-building process.

☑ We often act out of principles when we give others our trust.

☑ Having principles is critical for a successful business.

☑ Set clear boundaries in your life.

☑ Learn to be a person of principles.

KEY COMPONENT 7: ETHICS AND VALUES

DOING WHAT IS RIGHT OR WRONG + DOING WHAT WE VALUE

We often act out of ethics and values when we give others our trust. Let's talk about ethics first. Ethics matters. Ethics is not just a topic to mull over or debate. What is ethics? Ethics, or moral philosophy, is a discipline concerned with what is morally good or bad, right or wrong. Ethics deals with fundamental questions of practical decision-making, and its major concerns include the nature of ultimate value, and the standards by which human actions can be judged right or wrong.

Ethics gives solid, predictable direction. It is the guarantee of permanence, an integrity guideline and a moral compass. A moral compass is forever fixed and forever true. It's the golden rule for life.

People who live a life of ethical excellence base their worth on their values, possess an others-first mindset, sacrifice finances for family, and treat others with respect and dignity. What does the concept of ethics mean to you? Here are some possibilities:

- Ethics has to do with my religious beliefs.
- Ethics consists of the standards of behaviour our society accepts.
- Ethics has to do with what my feelings tell me is right or wrong.
- I don't know what the word means.

The reality is that the meaning of ethics is hard to explain, and the views many people have about ethics are shaky. Ethics has nothing to do with religion, and nor does it have anything to do with the standards of behaviour accepted by society in general. Ethics has nothing to do with your own feelings.

There are two other things you should know. First, ethics refers to well-founded standards of right and wrong. These standards prescribe what humans ought to do, usually in terms of rights, obligations, benefits to society, fairness, or specific virtues. Second, ethics refers to the study and development of personal ethical standards. Feelings, laws and social norms can deviate from what is ethical.

Values matter, too. What are values? Values reflect a person's sense of right and wrong or what 'ought' to be. Values can be defined as things that are important to us, valued by us. Values are the embodiment of what an organisation stands for, and should be the basis for the behaviour of its people.

'Ethics is knowing the difference between what you have a right to do and what is right to do.'

POTTER STEWART

Summary

☑ Ethics and values comprise the 7th Key Component of the trust-building process.

☑ We often act out of ethics and values when we give others our trust.

☑ Ethics matters and gives you a solid direction in your life.

☑ Values matter, too. Individually or organisationally, values determine what is right and what is wrong.

☑ Behaving ethically means acting in a manner consistent with what is right or moral.

28

KEY COMPONENT 8: INTENT AND PLANS

INTENT AND PLANS GROW OUT OF CHARACTER

What's your agenda? Out of what intent do you act? Rest assured, intent matters. Plans matter. What is intent, and what are plans? We all have certain motives, reasons for acting the way we do. We often act out of intent and plans when we give others our trust. Intent grows out of character. The problem is that we tend to judge ourselves by our intent, and others by their behaviour. We make a distinction between the two, which is not always fair.

Also, we tend to judge others' intent based on our own paradigms and experience. Our own perception of intent has a huge impact on trust. It is a good idea to inform people of your intent and plans. That will lead to trust.

Ask yourself what you can do to improve and better communicate your intent.

'Plans are only good intentions, unless they immediately degenerate into hard work.'

PETER DRUCKER

Summary

- [x] Intent and plans comprise the 8th Key Component of the trust-building process.

- [x] We often act out of intent and plans when we give others our trust.

- [x] We all have special motives for acting the way we do.

- [x] The greatest problem in communication is that we judge ourselves by our intent and others by their behaviour.

- [x] Genuinely caring about other people is the motive that inspires the greatest trust.

- [x] Your challenge is to improve your intentions and refine your motives.

KEY COMPONENT 9: ROUTINES

DESIGN YOUR PERFECT ROUTINE

Your daily routine can make a huge difference to how healthy, happy and productive you are. It is important to understand how the brain works and what kind of routine suits you best.

We often act out of routines when we give others our trust. What are routines? A routine is the daily flow of things that you have internalised in order to become successful. You have created procedures that you believe will make you more effective.

Here are the routines of two successful entrepreneurs:

- Jack Dorsey, Twitter and Square co-founder. Jack dedicates each day to a special theme:
  - Monday: management and running the company

- Tuesday: product
- Wednesday: marketing and communications, growth
- Thursday: developers and partnerships
- Friday: company culture and recruiting
- Saturday: hiking
- Sunday: reflections, feedback, strategy, getting ready for the new week

The advantages of Jack Dorsey's routine: Jack focuses on certain themes during the day, which means that he's not interrupted and can quickly find his way back to his focus.

- Leo Babauta, Zen Habits. Leo starts his day by planning what he wants to achieve. His morning routine:
  - Wake up at 4.30 am
  - Drink water
  - Schedule the three most important things for the day
  - Fix lunches for kids and himself
  - Eat breakfast, read
  - Exercise (run, bike, swim) or meditate
  - Shower
  - Wake wife and kids at 6.30 am

The advantages of Leo Babauta's routine: Leo is able to enjoy family life; find time for healthy eating, hygiene and fitness; and keep track of what he wants to achieve. Despite being busy in business, he is able to schedule enough time for family, leisure and health. Many entrepreneurs forget that being self-employed does not mean giving up everything for their business.

Do you have a daily routine? If not, be inventive and design your own routine that suits to your body. You must find out what suits you best. Here a few tips for designing your own daily routine:

- Enjoy a good and healthy breakfast
- Learn to go to bed with an alarm and wake up with an alarm
- Switch yourself off at night (zero notifications during the night)
- Track your habits

My routine consists of dedicating each day to two or three themes, like Jack Dorsey. This concept helps me staying focused.

'The secret of your future is hidden
in your daily routine.'

MIKE MURDOCK

Summary

☑ Routines are the 9th Key Component of the trust-building process.

☑ We often act out of routines when we give others our trust.

☑ It is an advantage to have daily routines.

☑ Routines help to get the best results from each day.

KEY COMPONENT 10: EXPERIENCE

OUR EXPERIENCES DEFINE US

Your traditions and habits all guide your decisions and experiences. Through your education, childhood and career, and in your surroundings and society, you are defined by your behaviour and principles. The way you are raised and educated, you tend to react and think. No matter what happens to you, your experiences define you.

We often act out of experience when we give others our trust. What are experiences? Experiences are events that have happened in the past, and the stories that make up your life. What is significant is the way you react to those experiences.

Do bad experiences make you feel dreary? Do you begin to doubt? Do you regret something? The best thing you can do is to learn from your experiences. If you learn from your experiences again and again, you will begin to grow and develop yourself further. And you overcome bad experiences.

'Experience is not, what happens to you.
It is, what you do with what happens to you.'

ALDOUS HUXLEY

Summary

☑ Experience is the 10th Key Component of the trust-building process.

☑ We often act out of experience when we give others our trust.

☑ All experiences, good or bad, define us.

☑ Think of experience as a chance to learn and grow.

31

KEY COMPONENT 11: SENSE OF DUTY

FEELING OBLIGED TO ACT IN A CERTAIN WAY

Sometimes you might find yourself acting with a strong sense of duty. What does sense of duty mean? Sense of duty is the feeling of being obliged to act in a certain way. Imagine the following scenario. You meet an old woman who wants to cross the road. She seems insecure, as though she has real problems. She's trembling and appears nervous. She looks helpless. Some possible reactions:

- You don't intend to help her.
- You see that she has a problem, but you don't have time to help.
- You encourage her to cross the road when the traffic lights are green for her.

- Out of sense of duty, you feel obliged to help her cross the road.

What does this example demonstrate? It shows that your life is defined by your experiences, where you are tested, where your sense of duty is tested. Helping the old woman is not something you *must* do. You are not obliged to help her. But a sense of duty can often be stronger than a lack of obligation. Helping the old woman gives you a good feeling, and she is happy, too.

> '*A good deed is not just a duty,*
> *but above all, a privilege.*'
>
> **SHARI ARISON**

Summary

☑ Sense of duty is the 11th Key Component of the trust-building process.

☑ We often act out of a sense of duty when we give others our trust.

☑ Sometimes your sense of duty is stronger than a lack of obligation.

☑ Helping or supporting someone else will leave you with a good feeling.

KEY COMPONENT 12: REASON

ACTING OBJECTIVELY

Sometimes we tend to rationalise our decisions in order to justify our behaviour. We often act out of reason when we give others our trust. What is reason? According to Wikipedia: 'Reason is the capacity for consciously making sense of things, establishing and verifying facts, applying logic, and changing or justifying practices, institutions, and beliefs based on new or existing information.'

You have probably learned to think logically in most situations, and apply the facts and information you have at the time. Acting with reason means that you don't lose sight of your ultimate goal. Reason gives your decisions quality and background.

Acting with reason means acting intelligently and objectively; acting with emotions can lead to a subjective action. In order to act with reason, you need to understand the issues you have to address.

> 'The reasonable man adapts himself to the world; the unreasonable one persists in trying to adapt the world to himself. Therefore all progress depends on the unreasonable man.'

GEORGE BERNARD SHAW

Summary

- ☑ Reason is the 12th Key Component of the trust-building process.
- ☑ We often act out of reason when we give others our trust.
- ☑ Acting with reason is the process of using intelligence and logical thinking, plus facts and information to come to a valuable decision.
- ☑ Reason gives your decisions quality and background.

33

KEY COMPONENT 13: SELF-ACTUALISATION

BECOME SELF-FULFILLED

We all want to reach our potential. It is only normal to strive for personal growth and self-actualisation. We often act out of self-actualisation when we give others our trust. What is self-actualisation? Abraham Maslow, in his hierarchy of needs, used this term to describe 'what a man can be, he must be. This need we may call self-actualisation'.

Self-actualisation can also been described as 'the psychological process aimed at maximizing the use of a person's abilities and resources. This process may vary from one person to another'.[3]

Self-actualisation means leveraging your abilities to reach your full potential. We all strive for self-fulfilment. Maslow said: '(a)

---

3   Couture et al, 2007.

musician must make music, an artist must paint, a poet must write, if he is to be ultimately happy.'

According to Albert Ellis, a humanistic psychologist, 'self-actualisation involves the pursuit of excellence and enjoyment; whichever people choose to desire and emphasize'.

> *'Every living organism is fulfilled, when it follows the right path for its own nature.'*
>
> **MARCUS AURELIUS**

Summary

☑ Self-actualisation is the 13th Key Component of the trust-building process.

☑ We often act out of self-actualisation when we give others our trust.

☑ Realising your potential is a personal endeavour that depends on where your creative, intellectual, or social potential lies.

☑ Self-actualisation is not about making the most money, or becoming the most famous person in the world. Self-actualisation is about the need for self-fulfilment.

☑ Self-actualisation is about reaching your full personal potential, whether that means becoming a painter, an artist, a teacher or anything else.

KEY COMPONENT 14: INTUITION

OUR GUT FEELING

We are living in a fast-paced world. We have learned to rely on the steady advancement of new technology. Ongoing research is working on developing technology that is more productive than our brains. A key question arises from this. Do we still need humans, or is artificial intelligence stronger? But there is one thing artificial intelligence is not capable of, and that is to think intuitively.

We often act out of intuition when we give others our trust. What is intuition? Intuition is the ability to understand something instinctively without the need for conscious reasoning. We are able to behave intuitively when we want to solve an unknown problem, but a computer cannot do that. Jack Welch, legendary CEO of General Electric, for example, has said that good decisions are made with just a gut feeling. Have you ever had a moment where you felt as though something wasn't right? A certain feeling without knowing why?

Where does intuition come from? Intuition begins with a process that results from given information, knowledge and experience. Neurons build an interpretation, which is expressed in a feeling.

Should we rely on our intuition? Even in issues of the utmost complexity, intuition can be a great help. Our gut feeling works best when we know a lot, but not everything. Even when important strategic decisions are to be made, thirty percent of entrepreneurs trust their intuition.

Experts often have the right gut feeling. They base this feeling on their experience. Human decisions will never be completely flawless, but with good gut feelings we can and do often achieve good solutions for problems.

'Your time is limited so don't waste it living someone else's life. Don't be trapped by dogma, which is living with the results of other people's thinking. Don't let the noise of others' opinions drown out your own inner voice. And most important, have the courage to follow your heart and intuition.'

STEVE JOBS

Summary

☑ Intuition is the 14th Key Component of the trust-building process.

☑ We often act out of intuition when we give others our trust.

☑ Intuition means we are able to understand things instinctively.

☑ You should take notice of your gut feelings more often.

PART IV

BECOMING A KEY PERSON OF TRUST

WHAT IS A KEY PERSON OF TRUST?

A BRANDING CONCEPT FOR MAXIMUM SUCCESS

Now that we have talked about the critical Key Components for building trust in detail, we can dive into the topic of becoming a Key Person of Trust (KPT). What exactly is a KPT and why do we need a new branding concept?

In the social media era, branding yourself is no longer optional. No matter what your business is, you need to create your own brand. Done right, branding can make you a successful entrepreneur.

Make sure you are on the right track with your personal brand-building efforts:

- Learn about trust and trustworthiness: If you want to have maximum success, a minimum of information about trust is no longer sufficient. You should have quality information about trust. You should know the background of trust, learn how to become trustworthy, learn the different personality types, adopt a new way of thinking, and modify your attitude and behaviour with regard to trust.
- Develop your personality further: Being good at what you do and working hard is no longer enough. If you want to be successful in the long run, you need to stand out and be recognised. You must convince with your personality, character and attitude.
- Develop your leadership further: It is not enough to convince with a great personality, leadership must be learned, too. If you want to be successful, you must be visible, valuable and connected. You must be a thought leader. You must be a trustworthy leader.
- Develop your brand: The end product is a reputable and respected brand. Such a brand demonstrates and spreads trust.

Requirement of a new branding concept

Maximum success in the long run needs a new branding concept, one that encompasses the topics of entrepreneurship, trust and branding. To be successful as an entrepreneur, you need to learn not only about branding, but about trust and entrepreneurship, too. The topic of trust is not usually a separate element in a branding concept.

Branding experts don't see this topic as worth mentioning. They only speak of the necessary brand trust, and that is all. But trust is becoming more and more important nowadays. Trust is so important that we really must talk about it separately.

Personal branding success is built on four pillars:

1. Trust
2. Personality
3. Leadership
4. Brand

The branding concept of 'Becoming a Key Person of Trust (KPT)' builds upon these four pillars.

What a Key Person of Trust is not

Being a KPT doesn't mean simply being more experienced or more likable than others. Experience and competency don't play a role in this concept, although these skills are definitely important in business in general. And popularity should never be your aim. Being liked is certainly fascinating, but when it comes to having success, too much focus on popularity can be harmful.

What a Key Person of Trust is really

A KPT can be characterised by certain Key Qualities that, taken together, lead to success. The 10 Key Qualities of a KPT:

1. Self-Trust + Self-Confidence
2. Authenticity/Credibility/Trustworthiness

3. Character + Attitude
4. Make a Difference/Know your Uniqueness + Distinctiveness
5. Learn to Present /Perform
6. Visibility/Attractiveness (for people, contacts and dream customers)
7. Develop a Personal Voice, Message, Mission and Vision
8. Create Chances + Opportunities/Get Orders easily
9. Good Reputation
10. More Trust + More Influence

See the infographic here:

10 KEY QUALITIES

THE NEXT REVOLUTION IN BRANDING
Becoming a Key Person of Trust
(KPT)

1.
SELF-TRUST + SELF CONFIDENCE

2.
AUTHENTICITY, CREDIBILITY, TRUSTWORTHINESS

3.
CHARACTER + ATTITUDE

4.
MAKE A DIFFERENCE / KNOW YOUR UNIQUENESS + DISTINCTIVENESS

5.
BE ABLE TO PRESENT / PERFORM

10 KEY QUALITIES

THE NEXT REVOLUTION IN BRANDING
Becoming a Key Person of Trust
(KPT)

6.
VISIBILITY + ATTRACTIVENESS

7.
OWN PERSONAL VOICE, MESSAGE, MISSION, VISION

8.
CREATE CHANCES + OPPORTUNITIES / GET ORDERS EASILY

9.
GOOD REPUTATION

10.
MORE TRUST + MORE INFLUENCE

We will discuss these points in detail later, but for now we can say that trust, personality, leadership and brand matter more than ever, and they are key to your success as an entrepreneur. The aim of this book is to offer you a useful guide to building your personal brand.

*'Becoming a Key Person of Trust is
the highlight of your business.'*

KARIN SEBELIN

Summary

☑ Becoming a KPT will lead to maximum business success, and a new chapter in your professional life.

☑ The branding concept KPT builds upon the four pillars: trust, personality, leadership and brand, and teaches the importance of certain Key Qualities that together lead to success.

☑ Trust plays an important role in business; this branding concept fosters trust and leads to long-term success.

TRUST ALONE IS NOT ENOUGH

TRUST VERSUS A KEY PERSON OF TRUST

We all know something about trust, but only something. In fact, we know so little that we're not always sure how to behave correctly. Trust in everyday life is a mix of feeling and rational thinking. One day you might act in a certain way, according to a gut feeling, and another day you will rationalise your decisions. You might be insecure, or have fear when it comes to trusting others. We, too often, don't follow concrete principles and have no real standard of behaviour.

Trust is a topic that involves many insecurities, problems and doubts. You need to know more about trust, and learn a new approach that will lead to maximum success. We need a concept; trust alone is not a concept. It is a word, a feeling.

Trust needs a concept. A new branding concept. To become successful in the long term we need a new branding concept that deals with trust in details, too.

This is where the concept of becoming a KPT comes into play. This concept will change the way we approach trust, branding and entrepreneurship. It encompasses the topics of entrepreneurship, trust and branding. Through this concept you will be able to transform yourself into a remarkable personality, a great leader, and a trusted and respected brand. All you need to do is learn about trust and focus on the Key Qualities that are important to be a KPT.

'Trust is not a concept; it is a feeling.'

KARIN SEBELIN

Summary

☑ As trust is a topic with no concept behind it, you must follow a concept to become successful in the long term.

☑ The branding concept of becoming a KPT deals with the details of trust.

☑ When you become a KPT, you learn the importance of trust and the Key Qualities that lead to maximum success in branding and business. Seize your chance and become successful using this concept.

37

DO YOU SELL TRUST?

THE RIGHT BRANDING
HELPS TO ADD VALUE

We all know what branding is. People often think that trust alone is the way to success. That is not totally false, but trust alone does not help sell products or services. With a great branding concept, you will be able to be more convincing. With the branding concept of becoming a KPT, you will be able to convince more. You will convince with trust, your personality, your leadership and ultimately your brand.

What is the consequence? A brand that can convince more can charge more for its product, even four to five times more than an equally reliable generic version of the same product. For example, with trust alone you might sell your product for $80; as a KPT you might be able to sell the same product for $400.

See the difference? It's a decisive difference. Good branding will help you to add value. Consumers look for the signs of a KPT, and they are generally happy to pay a lot more for that additional reliability. Thus, it makes good sense to become a KPT.

'Trust alone does not create customers.'

KARIN SEBELIN

Summary

☑ As a KPT, you can charge more for your services and products - you can convince more.

☑ Branding as a KPT will add value to your business.

☑ Trust alone does not sell products and services.

HABITS OF KEY PEOPLE OF TRUST

GOOD HABITS LEAD TO TRUST

Convincing in conversations depends on what you say and how you communicate your message. It also depends on your behaviour and how you treat other people. There are people in our world who win over everyone with their personality, character and attitude.

One quality of a KPT is that they attract people to them. How do they do that? They are either born with a certain instinct, have a special feeling for people, or have learned to incorporate the concept of KPT.

Let's have a deeper look at why KPTs draw people to them. KPTs have special routines that become habits. Common traits of KPTs:

- Are extremely polite
- Acknowledge small favours
- Offer meaningful praise/compliments
- Express sincere empathy
- Share useful information
- Are very supportive
- Use names and titles to demonstrate respect
- Express their faith in others

Good habits lead to trust and good relationships. KPTs convince with good habits and good behaviour.

'Good habits are the key to all success.'

OG MANDINO

Summary

☑ KPTs are able to draw people to them.

☑ KPTs have learned that sound habits, respectful handling of other people and good behaviour lead to trust.

WHAT IS AN ENTREPRENEUR?

ENTREPRENEURS CHANGE THE WORLD

Entrepreneurs can change the way we live and work. Their innovations can improve standard of living, and create jobs, and set the conditions for prosperous societies. Entrepreneurs create new businesses. We all know famous entrepreneurs: Steve Jobs, Richard Branson, Mark Zuckerberg quickly come to mind. We all know the stories about them:

- Former CEO of Apple, Steve Jobs invented the iPad, iPod and the iPhone. He founded his company in 1976 by selling motherboards.
- Richard Branson, CEO of the Virgin Group, started his business at the age of sixteen in the form of a magazine called *Student*, and followed on to found Virgin Records.

- Mark Zuckerberg, CEO of Facebook, revolutionised social networking. He started his business in his college dormitory room in 2004.

What is an entrepreneur? An entrepreneur is a person who starts a new business venture. Is a small-business owner an entrepreneur, too? Every entrepreneur is a small-business owner, but not every small-business owner is an entrepreneur. There are different types of entrepreneurs:

- Small-business entrepreneur: This category includes local business owners. Small-businesses can include partnerships, sole proprietors and LLCs. In general, small businesses have less than five hundred employees.
- Home-based business: A business that is run from home.
- Online-business entrepreneur: These businesses can be internet based, and either small, home-based businesses or large corporations.
- Inventor: This type of entrepreneur needs to go beyond the idea stage to build the product and get it to the market. A good example is the TV show *Shark Tank*, wherein budding entrepreneurs with creative ideas for new businesses make their pitch on national television to a tough audience of successful businesspeople.
- Serial entrepreneur: These people get the most joy out of starting and building up new businesses, and even by eventually selling them. Serial entrepreneurs often juggle several businesses at once.

Here are some general characteristics of entrepreneurs:

- Passionate/enthusiastic
- Optimistic/believe in themselves
- Convince with self-confidence
- Resilient: failure is not a problem for them, and they are happy to learn from setbacks and move on
- Focused/concentrate on the important details
- Doers/action oriented
- Convince with independent thinking/think outside the box
- Disciplined/willing to work hard
- Visionaries; they dream big (see Richard Branson, Jeff Bezos, Elon Musk, Thomas Edison)
- Problem solvers (see Henry Ford)
- Have talent for seeing opportunities and the ability to develop those opportunities into profit-making businesses/create their own success
- Great team leaders who build and surround themselves with great teams

You don't need to have all these traits associated with entrepreneurship in order to be successful. Dale Carnegie, famous communicator, motivational trainer and author of the bestseller *How to Win Friends and Influence People*, said: 'Flaming enthusiasm, backed up by horse sense and persistence, is the quality that most frequently makes for success.'

The ability to express your enthusiasm and instil it in others is the key to turning your ideas into reality. Entrepreneurs are bold people. They live their dreams and prove to others that by taking the necessary steps they can make these dreams happen. There is a saying: 'People don't get enthused by your idea, people get enthused by you.' This means you must convince with your personality and attitude, and not only with your idea.

Johann Wolfgang von Goethe, famous 19th-century German poet and philosopher, said: 'Whatever you can do or dream you can, begin it. Boldness has genius, power and magic in it. Begin it now.' His advice for would-be entrepreneurs is excellent.

The main qualities you need as entrepreneur to make your business venture succeed:

- Strong determination
- Bold commitment
- Enthusiasm
- Passion

There are no excuses left for you now. You don't need to be superhuman; you only need a simple idea, and it doesn't even need to be original. Develop your vision, and communicate it to others with boldness. Learn how to infect others with your enthusiasm for your idea. Your success lies in implementing your idea, and then in the execution of your plans.

Do you want to be a successful entrepreneur? Becoming an entrepreneur is not hard, but it needs work. Develop the above mentioned traits. Come up with a great idea, and then execute your plan with consistency.

There are a few common misconceptions about entrepreneurs: People often think they are wild risk-takers, but that's not true. Entrepreneurs do take risks, but only calculated ones. They have the ability to evaluate risks.

Are entrepreneurs born or made? Some business experts believe that the entrepreneurial drive is innate, a trait acquired at birth, while others believe that anyone can become an entrepreneur. We could say that some people are naturally more entrepreneurial than others.

'I never dreamed about success. I worked for it.'

ESTÉE LAUDER

Summary

- ☑ An entrepreneur is a person who starts a new business venture.

- ☑ Some people are born with entrepreneurial skills, but anyone can become an entrepreneur.

- ☑ Becoming an entrepreneur takes work and requires skills that can be developed.

- ☑ An entrepreneur should be committed, and have strong determination, enthusiasm and passion in order to succeed. Entrepreneurs also need focus, optimism, self-confidence, resilience, independent thinking, work ethics, vision, problem-solving ability, be orientated toward action, and the ability to create opportunities and great teams.

- ☑ Entrepreneurship is about working for success, not only dreaming about success.

WHAT IS A BRAND/ WHAT IS BRANDING?

BRAND AND BRANDING DEFINED

We all know something about brand and branding, but many people think only of logos when they hear the word *branding*. Logos are only one part of the brand-building process, and logos are only one expression of a brand. There are many things that go into the brand-building process.

What is a brand? Branding experts like Philip Kotler and Gary Armstrong say that a brand is 'a name, term, sign, or symbol (or combination of these) that identifies the maker or seller of the product'. Marty Neumeier says that a brand is 'a person's gut feeling about a product, service, or organisation'.

Your brand is an authentic expression of your company as you present it to the world, built on the foundation of your perspective and your personality. 'Your brand is defined by a customer's overall perception of your business,' according to Sonia Gregory.

A strong brand describes a company or person that has chosen to make a meaningful difference in the lives of others, and that builds trusting and valued relationships. For me personally, a brand is a name with the power to influence. There are three important kinds of brands in the world of business and entrepreneurship:

1. Product brand
2. Company brand
3. Personal brand

Our focus in this discussion is on personal brand. To illustrate the difference, Elon Musk is a personal brand, Tesla is a company brand, and Model 3, Model X and Model S are product brands.

Why is just a personal brand so important? Many small businesses focus on big businesses and take note of what they are doing. They might put huge effort in creating a company or product brand, but what is most important is the personal brand. Why? In public, we recognise names, faces and the sound of people's voices first, and only then do we recognise logos, colours and symbols.

Qualities of strong brands:

- Distinctive: the brands stand for something
- Relevant: the brands build relevance through having a stake in others' needs and interests
- Consistent: doing things that are distinctive and relevant over and over again

Strong brands stand out in a densely crowded marketplace. Brands have three primary functions:

1. Navigation: brands help consumers choose from a wide selection of choices
2. Reassurance: brands communicate the decisive quality of the products and services, and reassure customers that they have made the right decision
3. Engagement: brands use distinctive imagery, communication and associations to encourage customers to identify with the brand

Here are two examples of successful brands: Volvo is known for its safety records, and Toyota is known for its reliability. Each of these companies has built their brand to be easily recognisable and appeal to their customers in a unique way.

What is branding? According to Kotler & Keller (2015), 'branding is endowing products and services with the power of a brand'. Branding is the process of giving meaning to a specific company, products and services by creating and shaping a brand in the mind of the consumer. It gives personality to a company, and attaches an attribute to the company name that appeals to the demographic of its core audience.

Branding is also a strategy that companies design to help people quickly identify their products, services and organisation; it gives the customer a reason to choose their products and services over the competition by clarifying what this brand is and is not.

Your own branding will tell consumers what they can expect of you, and what they will experience when utilising your products or services. Branding is a disciplined process for building awareness and extending customer loyalty.

'Brand is not, what you say it is.
It's what they say it is.'

MARTY NEUMEIER, *THE BRAND GAP*

'Businesses are only as strong as their brands.'

KARIN SEBELIN

Summary

☑ A product or service is what you sell, a brand is the perceived image of that, and branding is the strategy to create that image.

☑ Branding is how you can establish an image of your company in your customers' eyes. Become a great brand and invest in a great (personal) branding.

☑ Strong brands are distinctive, relevant and consistent. They stand out in the marketplace.

THE DIFFERENCE BETWEEN MARKETING AND BRANDING

THE CONFUSION BETWEEN MARKETING AND BRANDING

Marketing and branding are buzzwords that we use in the industry. There is a distinctive difference between marketing and branding that I will explain here, because these terms are often confused. So what is the major difference between marketing and branding? Branding is the strategy, while marketing represents the tactical goals. Branding is strategic, and marketing is tactical. Marketing refers to the tools you utilise to deliver your brand message.

You might argue that tactics and strategy are the same, but they are not. Brand loyalty will remain long after a marketing campaign has been exhausted. Marketing gets in and convinces the customer of the benefits of a particular product. It doesn't try to direct the user's long-term feelings towards the product. Your brand image needs to be cultivated in such a way that the customer associates an idea, emotion or connection with your brand.

Branding is a long-term concept; marketing is more short term. Branding is about building brand loyalty and trust; marketing is necessary to make good branding work. Your real benefit, however, is brand loyalty.

Marketing is always a good investment. It offers great opportunities, and can be performed through a variety of online and offline methods. Some of the most common:

- SEO
- Content marketing
- Social media marketing
- Pay-per-click marketing
- Mobile marketing
- Television/radio
- Print campaigns

Marketing can be a mix of text, keywords, photos, infographics, charts and videos. It can be serious, heartfelt or funny. As times have changed and new technologies came up, we cannot do our marketing in the same way like years ago. Traditional marketing does not work anymore.

Businesses must embrace change if they want to be successful. They should also look for creative ways to succeed, for instance, by tapping into new marketing tactics, trying new things and adopting new technologies. If you want to be successful, you should always consider the value of trust, which will always play a great role in success.

Marketing can easily be done wrong, and it can be a money sink. However, well-researched marketing generally gives a great return on investments, and branding is usually easier to adjust as time goes by.

Which comes first, marketing or branding? If you are a beginning entrepreneur, it's essential to clearly define who you are as a brand, before you begin to define your specific marketing methods, tools, strategies and tactics. Your brand is what will keep your clients coming back for more. Your marketing methods may evolve, responding to current industry and cultural trends, but your branding will remain the same.

Keep in mind that branding is something you and your team must do on a daily basis.

'Marketing is too important to be left to the marketing department.'

DAVID PACKARD

Summary

☑ Branding is strategic, whereas marketing is tactical.

☑ Marketing is necessary, no question, but marketing by itself can't develop an audience interested in your message.

☑ Branding makes your audience interested in your message.

☑ Branding is about building brand loyalty and trust.

☑ Invest time and money in great branding, but don't forget to do the right marketing. Be aware that traditional marketing does not work anymore. In times of change and new technology, businesses must adapt or die.

☑ Use marketing to develop your branding, but don't forget the difference between the two.

☑ Branding is something you should concentrate on daily.

☑ Branding is long term; marketing is more short term.

WHY BRANDING?

NEVER UNDERESTIMATE GOOD BRANDING

Branding is becoming more and more important nowadays. We have to acknowledge that we live in a branded world. The concept of personal branding gained currency in the late 1990s, after a cover story titled 'The Brand Called You', written by Tom Peters and published in the magazine *Fast Company*. Peters wrote: 'To be in business today, our most important job is to be head marketer for the brand called You ... Everyone has a chance to learn, improve, and build up their skills. Everyone has a chance to be a brand worthy of remark.'

Starting today with your business, you are a brand. Branding is not just for companies. Each of us has a personal brand that can be seen in places like Instagram, Snapchat, Twitter, and Facebook feeds. We are living increasingly digital lives. Our selfies, comments and stories represent our brand. Each of us stands for something, regardless of whether we are entrepreneurs, food bloggers or nerds.

Branding is just as important for small businesses as it is for big companies. Never underestimate the value of good branding. Many entrepreneurs and business owners understand very well that branding is essential to their business, but a surprisingly high number of them don't really know why that is.

Building a successful brand is about more than designing a cool-looking logo. Branding is not just a logo, or the way a business is perceived externally. It is a way of defining the business, the team, and any external audiences. Branding is the business's identity.

Ten reasons why branding is so important for your business:

1. Branding sets your business apart from the competition: In today's world and global market, it is critical to stand out from the crowd. Businesses are no longer competing on a local stage but in the global economy, competing with the whole world. How can you stand out from the thousands of similar organisations around the world? What makes you unique and valuable to others? How do you want to be perceived?

2. Good branding helps give your business value well beyond any physical assets: Think about brands like Coca-Cola and Apple. Are these companies really worth their equipment, products, warehouses and/or factories? These companies are worth much more than their physical assets; their brand has created a value that far exceeds their physical value. What does your business value look like?

3. Branding tells people about your business's DNA: Your full brand experience, from the visual elements like your logo to the way

you communicate with others, tells people what kind of company you are. Are you telling the right story?

4. Branding helps others know what to expect from you: Good branding that is consistent and clear puts prospective customers at ease because they know exactly what to expect each and every time they experience your brand. What can people expect from you?

5. Branding reflects you and your promise to your customers: Keep in mind that your brand represents you. You and your staff are the brand, and your marketing materials are also the brand. What are you delivering (promising) to your customers?

6. Branding promotes recognition: People tend to do business with companies they are familiar with; companies they like and trust. If your branding is consistent and easy to recognise, it can help people feel more at ease purchasing your products or services. What do you do to gain recognition?

7. A strong brand generates referrals: People love to tell other people about the brands they like, and about their experiences with different brands. Today we all wear brands, eat brands and listen to brands, and we're constantly telling others about the brands we love. On the flip side, we also tend to criticise those brands we don't like. Word of mouth is a powerful tool to improve brand recognition. A strong brand is critical to generating referrals. How do you create referrals?

8. Branding helps you connect with people: A strong brand connects with people at an emotional level. They feel good when they are around the brand, and interact with and buy the brand. Purchasing is an emotional experience, and good branding can support this experience. What kind of emotions do you bring to the table?

9. A strong brand provides motivation and direction for others: A clear brand strategy provides the clarity you need to be successful. A strong brand delivers motivation and direction for others. It can inspire people. How do you motivate and inspire others?

10. Branding helps you create clarity and stay focused: Good branding can guide you; a clear brand strategy helps you stay focused on your mission and vision, as a personality and as an organisation. Branding can help you be strategic and guide your marketing efforts, saving time and money. The best branding is built on a strong concept, an idea that you and your staff can hold onto, can commit to, and can deliver on. What does your concept look like?

Good branding doesn't just happen. It takes strategy. It takes a concept. The concept of Key Person of Trust (KPT) can help you to success. Our branding services use a combination of research, experience, creativity, innovation and consulting to uncover your potential. We learn who you are, what you stand for, and where you're going. We teach you branding strategies that are based on the four pillars: trust, personality, leadership and brand.

Our branding concept for becoming a KPT is designed for maximum and long-term success. What is your brand's story?

'Personal branding is not about you.
It's about putting your stamp on the
value you deliver to others.'

WILLIAM ARRUDA

Summary

☑ Never underestimate the value of good branding.

☑ Invest time and money in a great brand personality, brand leadership and brand.

YOUR BRAND SNAPSHOT

WHERE YOU ARE RIGHT NOW

Before you get started with branding, you need to know where you are right now. Start by taking a quick inventory (brand snapshot) of what your brand looks like today. This will act as your starting point for moving forward. Here are some questions to ask yourself (be honest with your answers):

- How is my business today?
- Do I have enough customers?
- Are my sales numbers where I want them to be?
- Who are my customers?
- What do I know about my customers?
- How does my brand look, feel and sound to the outside world?

- What story am I telling?
- What do my current brand assets look like (logo, website, social media accounts, printed materials, marketing campaigns)?
- What would I change if I could?
- What do I like about my brand's presentation?

THE WRONG ATTITUDE TO SUCCESS

THERE IS NO SUCH THING AS OVERNIGHT SUCCESS

There are books on Amazon with titles that incorporate the words: *How to be an overnight success*. Such books imply that success can indeed happen overnight. Do you want to be an overnight success? Do you believe in miracles?

Being an entrepreneur has nothing to do with being successful overnight. Entrepreneurship is all about hard work, and continuing to work hard regardless of how many times you fail. For example, take Gary Vaynerchuk, CEO of VaynerMedia and chairman of VaynerX, who worked extremely hard to become so successful. People may think he was simply lucky, but he denied that idea with these words in a blog post: 'Nothing happens overnight. When people tell me I'm lucky that I've had so much luck, I get so frustrated. Luck has nothing to do with it. I worked weekends and holidays every day starting at fourteen years old to make this happen. I think back to all the time I put in of real, hard work, before I saw any of the benefits.'

The big problem is that people have no patience. They want to be successful immediately. It is certainly true that entrepreneurs have wonderful tools at their disposal these days to build, market and promote their brands. And some entrepreneurs have seemingly skyrocketed onto the scene and are taking the world by storm with their personality, leadership, brand, books, or any other product they are selling.

Just because we are able to do things faster than in former times thanks to current tools and communication channels, that does not mean there is such a thing as an 'overnight success'. If you dig a little deeper into the stories of these overnight successes, you will realise that they were years in the making.

What does success mean for you? What does it look like? Making a big impact with your thoughts and ideas? Impressing many people? Earning big money? Let us be clear: success is a journey, not a goal. And I repeat: there is no such thing as overnight success.

When you steadily aim for results, on achieving something, you will find no success. You don't need to pressure yourself to compete, to win, to come out on top. The truth is you cannot control the outcome. You cannot control anything except yourself. The only things you truly have control over are your attitude, your mindset, and your actions. The rest is out of your hands.

What is the difference between good and bad writers, good and bad CEOs, good and bad singers and athletes? The difference is that the good ones practise consistently. They focus on the process of getting better, every single day. By focusing on the process—doing the work, day in and day out—they become stronger, faster, more focused, and more skilled. True champions focus on the process. Ordinary people focus only on the outcome.

Some tips for success:

- Know your purpose: What are you searching for? What do you want to achieve and why? John C Maxwell, bestselling author and leadership coach, said: 'Success is knowing your purpose, growing to reach your maximum potential and sowing seeds that benefit others.'
- Develop yourself further: Concentrate on one main goal. Improve yourself continuously. Forget the past and focus on the future.
- Create something of value: Becoming a successful entrepreneur is a big undertaking, and there is considerable work to do.
- Help other people achieve success (plant seeds of value): Winston Churchill said: 'We make a living by what we get. But we make a life by what we give.'

*'Success is not a destination, but
the road that you're on.'*

MARLON WAYANS

Summary

- ☑ Forget aiming on becoming an overnight success; there is no such thing.

- ☑ Success is about hard work. Success is a journey, not a goal.

- ☑ True winners focus on the process, not the outcome.

WHAT CAN WE LEARN FROM SILICON VALLEY?

SILICON VALLEY IS A MINDSET

Entrepreneurs can find great inspiration by studying the stories of the many successful companies in Silicon Valley. What is Silicon Valley? It is an area of the San Francisco Bay area, specifically the Santa Clara Valley, that is home to many successful companies. SV serves as the global centre for high technology, venture capital, innovation, and social media.

According to Wikipedia, San José is the largest city; other major Silicon Valley cities include Palo Alto, Santa Clara, Mountain View and Sunnyvale. The San José metropolitan area has the third highest GDP per capita in the world (after Zurich in Switzerland and Oslo in Norway). Silicon Valley is one of the most significant locations of the high-tech industry in the world.

Some of the biggest companies in Silicon Valley:

- Apple
- AMD
- Hewlett Packard
- Cisco
- Google
- NVIDIA
- Facebook
- Oracle
- TESLA
- Symantec
- Intel
- eBay

What makes Silicon Valley so special? Why are companies so successful there? The answer is that it has a social and business ethos that supports innovation and entrepreneurship. Silicon Valley is not a geographical place, it's a mindset.

Here are four top tips for what you can learn from Silicon Valley:

1. Find a great coach/mentor: As Eric Schmidt, ex-executive chairman of Google, said so well, 'Everyone needs a coach.' Entrepreneurs shouldn't attempt to go it alone. They should find mentors. Even if you know your company and market better than anyone else in the world, a good outside perspective from someone will keep you focused and hone your skills.

2. Have a compelling vision and elevator pitch: It's often not the best ideas that take off (and raise the most capital); rather, it's the founders who best inspire customers, employees and even investors with their vision for growth and success. Find an elevator pitch so simple that someone could explain your product and vision to family and friends over dinner.

3. Constantly learn, evolve and innovate (creating a winning product is not enough): Because competition is fierce, entrepreneurs must constantly update their offers if they don't want to lose market share to their rivals. If you don't innovate, you will quickly become irrelevant. Silicon Valley teaches us that we must keep pace because business models are changing faster than ever.

4. It's all about humanity and relationships: Businesses nowadays need to show that they are problem-solvers, they make life easier for people, and they are able to form relationships. Entrepreneurs must have a human mission.

'Silicon Valley is a mindset, not a location.'

REID HOFFMAN

Summary

- ☑ Learn to think big like the entrepreneurs of Silicon Valley.
- ☑ Learn to follow your goals long term.
- ☑ Find a great coach/mentor.
- ☑ Have a compelling vision and elevator pitch.
- ☑ Constantly learn, evolve and innovate.
- ☑ Show your humanity and value your relationships.

46

KEY QUALITIES OF A KEY PERSON OF TRUST

DEFINITIONS – ANALYSIS – APPROACHES – FACTS

Now that we have talked about the things we should know, in order to be best prepared for trust, entrepreneurship, branding, marketing and success we can dive into the critical Key Qualities of a Key Person of Trust:

1. Self-Trust + Self-Confidence
2. Authenticity/Credibility/Trustworthiness
3. Character + Attitude
4. Make a Difference/Know your Uniqueness + Distinctiveness

5. Learn to Present /Perform
6. Visibility/Attractiveness (for people, contacts and dream customers)
7. Develop a Personal Voice, Message, Mission and Vision
8. Create Chances + Opportunities/Get Orders easily
9. Good Reputation
10. More Trust + More Influence

(See the infographic in chapter 35.)
Now, let's get to know these Key Qualities in detail.

KEY QUALITY 1: SELF-TRUST + SELF-CONFIDENCE

MORE SELF-TRUST. MORE SELF-CONFIDENCE. MORE SUCCESS.

In order to have success in life it is important that you conquer your fears and develop self-trust. Self-trust, confidence and motivation will give you the needed energy and focus to work on your success. Self-trust will be harnessed when you follow your own sacred wisdom instead of looking steadily outside yourself.

When children are raised in an environment where they do not doubt themselves, self-trust can unfold successfully. In such an environment, children can feel completely accepted without judgement or conditions.

Every child needs a little guidance to help them understand and recognise their own strengths; they can then trust their own abilities. Parents should guide their children to look within themselves for answers. This is the process of teaching self-trust.

We develop self-trust by honouring our emotions and innermost thoughts instead of hiding behind them. Honouring our feelings is very important in life, and means that we can develop trust in our capacity to deal with whatever arises. On the other hand, we must distance ourselves from people who undermine our self-trust. People who steadily discourage us are harmful for our self-trust.

Learn from my story. When I founded my company, Presse-Service Karin Sebelin, several years ago, I was fortunate enough to have two freelance jobs, one as an editor and another as a copy editor. And it was fine like that. It gave me enough self-confidence to walk my own path, and it also made it easier for customers to reach me.

I have gained more success by having more confidence. One of my secrets of success is having a good dose of self-trust and self-confidence, which is the basis of everything or, as I put it, the foundation for building trust.

Our demeanour, thoughts and actions, and also our successes and even our failures—they all enhance our self-image, provided we do not let our setbacks and failures pull us down. Instead, we should see them as opportunities for learning and personal development.

Your own image of yourself is the basis for the external image; that is, the image that others have of you. If you present a positive self-image other people will also perceive you positively.

*'Self-trust and self-confidence
are the basis of branding.'*

KARIN SEBELIN

Summary

☑ The 1st Key Quality of a Key Person of
Trust is self-trust and self-confidence.

☑ You need self-trust and self-confidence
for success.

QUESTIONNAIRE

IDENTIFY YOUR CURRENT BALANCE OF SELF-DOUBT AND SELF-TRUST

This questionnaire will help you identify your current balance of self-doubt and self-trust. Answer the following questions and give yourself a score, where 0 means it doesn't apply at all, and 5 reflects a feeling or behaviour that often affects you.

1. Do you often sacrifice your own needs for others?
2. Do you doubt that you are capable of reaching a particular goal?
3. Do you hide your own mistakes?
4. Do you long to do something big (e.g. write a book), but doubt your ability?
5. Are you afraid of failing in life or business?
6. Do you give up too quickly when difficulties arise?
7. Do you regret events that have happened?

8. Do you often change your opinion?
9. Do you easily lose motivation?
10. Do you envy others for being more successful?

Add up the points to find your awareness score: 20 points or more means that your current state of thinking and behaviour needs some improvement and change.

49

SELF-CONFIDENCE TRUMPS INTELLIGENCE

SUCCESS DEPENDS ON SELF-CONFIDENCE AND PERSONALITY

Successful people don't always have special know-how or skills when it comes to business. They can often be effective by using their personality alone, plus a specific set of character traits and self-confidence.

IQ is largely fixed, but personality can be changed. A bad personality need not be your destiny. You can work on your personality and improve it.

Don't ask yourself: 'Do I have the brains to succeed?' It's better to ask yourself: 'Do I have the character to succeed?' You don't have to be the next Einstein to have success.

Self-confidence and personality trump intelligence. Do you know that self-confidence is contagious? Confident people inspire confidence in others: in their audience, their customers and their friends. Learn to be self-confident. Look at what you have already achieved. Think about your strengths and what you want to achieve in the future. Commit yourself to success.

Do you know how confident you seem to others, how you are perceived by them? Are you shy or anxious? Do you come over as doubting? Low self-esteem can be self-destructive. Confident people are generally more positive. They believe in themselves and their abilities.

'A man cannot be comfortable
without his own approval.'

MARK TWAIN

Summary

- ☑ Success is not about intelligence.
- ☑ Develop your self-confidence and personality.
- ☑ Be aware of your personality and self-confidence.
- ☑ Change the things about yourself that hinder your success.
- ☑ Work on your character, attitude and self-confidence.

50

TWENTY-ONE WAYS TO BOOST SELF-CONFIDENCE

SELF-CONFIDENCE CAN HELP ACCOMPLISH GOALS

Self-confidence can help you to succeed. It can help you build strong relationships. But the reverse is also true: a lack of self-confidence can be harmful to your success. Fortunately, you can boost your self-confidence. Nobody is born with limitless self-confidence. Anyone who has incredible self-confidence has undoubtedly worked on building it for years.

Here are twenty-one things you can do to boost your self-confidence:

1. Visualise yourself and how you want to be: Napoleon Hill said: 'What the mind can conceive and believe it can achieve.' Visualisation is a great technique for leading you to success. Seeing an image of yourself that you are proud of will give you security and optimism. Practise visualising yourself now, and how you want to be.

2. Use the power of affirmations: Affirmations are positive and uplifting statements that you tell yourself repeatedly. Exercise every day, and say to yourself: 'I am a winner. I will succeed.' You will see that this works wonders."

3. Do one thing that scares you every day: We should all learn to face our fears. Get out of your comfort zone and do something that scares you every day. Gain confidence from this experience.

4. Become addicted to premieres: A few suggestions for first-time experiences:
   - Visit a museum or fair
   - Attend a conference
   - Begin a new project
   - Go out for dinner with someone spontaneously
   - Take a holiday that is different from your usual kind, e.g. backpacker, luxury travel, Airbnb, or travel to a country that is new to you
   - Try a new sport

5. Soothe your inner critic: Sometimes our inner critic can be our worst enemy. Struggling with self-confidence can mean that your inner critic is too active, so find opportunities to reward yourself, even for small successes.

6. Set yourself up to win: Set yourself small goals that you can win easily. When you have achieved something, move on to a harder goal. Keep a list of all your achievements, no matter how large or small.

7. Help others: Helping other people enables us to forget about ourselves. We then feel grateful for what we have. It always feels good when we can make a difference in someone else's life. By assisting others, you'll see your self-confidence grow.

8. Practise self-care: Self-care is nothing selfish. Our self-confidence depends largely on a combination of good health of every kind: emotional, social and physical. Only when you feel good about yourself will you be able to show self-confidence. Find time to cultivate a workout routine, and develop good eating and sleeping habits. And dress nicely.

9. Learn to say no: Accept no one else's definition of your life; define yourself. Teach others to respect your personal boundaries. Learn to have control over your life.

10. Show a clear attitude to life and values: Insist on your own principles and values, and have a clear idea of how you perceive your life and success. Don't let others dictate your life. It is *your* life.

11. Be a positive role model when it comes to behaviour: Inspire others through your behaviour. Encourage other people. Live trust.

12. Smile: The quickest way to change your mood for the better and thus get more self-confidence is to smile spontaneously. Why does it work? The mind is connected to the body and one affects the other. Try it for yourself. Smile right now, and be amazed at the immediate positive effect it has on your mood.

13. Breathe consciously: Conscious breathing will relax you and free you, and make you feel self-confident. As soon as you realise that you're feeling excited or nervous, try the following:
   ▪ Breathe deeply into the abdomen intently for several breaths.

- Slow your breathing and breathe deeply into the lower part of the abdomen.
- Be aware of your breathing.
- Feel how your stomach is expanding.
- Breathe evenly and slowly.

14. Posture: Learn to improve your posture. Be aware of yourself. Straighten your spine, and hold your head up with your eyes straight ahead, your shoulders down, and your chest out. Think of yourself as being ten percent larger than you are, and hold this attitude as strongly and steadily as possible. A better and more conscious posture makes you more confident.

15. Be energetic: Self-confident people appear energetic. They know where they want to go. Have a firm step and a safe walk.

16. Do sports: Take more time for your body. If you are in an energy hole, you cannot feel safe. You feel lethargic and impotent. Get out in the open air more often and do some sports. Go jogging, walking, cycling or just take a walk. Or go to the gym and do strength training regularly. You will feel much better when you do: stronger, with more energy and love of life. Not only will it get your body moving, but you will also be doing something for your digestion and health. There is nothing better than sports.

17. Sit in the first row: In schools, lecture halls and meeting rooms, we humans have the habit of gravitating toward the back rows. We are afraid to be noticed; we prefer to stay invisible. Such behaviour does not promote self-esteem. Do not be one of these people. Dare to choose the front seats and show self-confidence.

18. Say what you think more often: It is unbelievable how few people actually open their mouths and say what they think. Most just sit there, afraid to say something wrong and possibly to be ridiculed by others. This fear is totally overrated. The people around you

are probably more open than you think. If you want to get ahead in life, open your mouth and give your opinion. Say what you think about the topic. Do not hesitate. Be self-confident.

19. Be grateful: Gratitude is one of the most important elements in life. Those who are grateful for their lives and accomplishments become humble and learn to be satisfied with less. Think about what you're thankful for. Focus on the things that are really great in your life, that you can be positive and optimistic about. What do you appreciate about life? What have you already achieved? The little things in life are often the best. Small moments are often worth more than all the money in the world. Learn to be grateful and appreciate your life.

20. Compliment your fellow human beings: If you are not satisfied with yourself you could be projecting that onto other people. This negative behaviour will not take you one step further, and instead you will sink ever deeper into negative feelings. Stop this behaviour and get used to not transferring your own dissatisfaction onto others. Most of the time, other people will not be responsible for whatever it is that you are feeling. Praise your fellow human beings often, compliment them and cheer them up. If you consistently try to see the best in others, indirectly you will be bringing out the best in yourself. Complimenting other people will contribute significantly to improving your mood.

21. Contribute something to this world: There is hardly a better feeling than having a meaning in life. Making a difference, being important to other people, contributing to our society ... unfortunately we are often too busy with ourselves, with our own wishes and needs. Start focusing on what you can give to this world and the people around you. Your confidence will

increase and you will enjoy the feeling of having contributed, being important to someone and making a difference. The more you give to this world and your fellow human beings, the more you will get back in the end.

'*Low self-esteem is like driving through life with your hand brake on.*'

MAXWELL MALTZ

Summary

☑ Boost your self-confidence.

☑ Be inventive in finding ways to express yourself.

☑ Practise every day.

SELF-CONFIDENCE + PERSONAL STYLE = TRUST

FIND YOUR PERSONAL STYLE

Clothes can influence how you are perceived. A suit that does not fit your personality can adversely affect other people's perception of you. Colours, the kind of cloth, patterns, and the style of your clothing can add to a positive self-image. A false colour could make you look dreary and insignificant. How do you want to be perceived? Here are three inspirational ideas for improving your personal style:

1. The power of choice: You dress and beautify your body, so you alone are in charge of how you appear to observers. You can choose what you want to express and what you want to hide,

what you want to display and what to mask. There is a lot of power in clothes and style. Why not take the opportunity to broadcast a few key pieces of information about yourself through your appearance? Build self-confidence and pride, establish your uniqueness, and highlight important aspects of your inner life.

2. Show respect for yourself: In dressing with care and sensitivity, you broadcast respect for yourself. Dressing with care means finding the perfect clothes for the day's activities, clothes that fit well and suit your unique figure. Dressing with care is about making sartorial choices that will showcase your best self. When you dress to show respect for yourself the people around you cannot help but sense your self-confidence. If you want people to respect you, first you must respect yourself.

3. Look good to feel good: Did you know that there is a connection between looking good and feeling good? If you look bad you will feel bad. Why is that? The answer is rooted in perception. If you see yourself in the mirror wearing a dreary outfit, how could you find yourself attractive? Conversely, if you wear a lovely outfit you will begin to admire yourself. You will find joy and happiness when you see yourself. Use personal style as a tool for cultivating self-care and reflecting self-respect. Learn to flatter your figure. Utilise your natural beauty to reflect your amazing self outward to the observing world. Doing something for your personal style and improving your outer appearance will help you gain self-confidence and can lead to more success.

There is an equation: Self-Confidence + Personal Style = Trust.

'The key to personal style is understanding your individual beauty enough to know, which looks will work for you and which probably won't.'

STACY LONDON

Summary

☑ Challenge yourself to constantly play with colours, prints, fabrics and silhouettes.

☑ Try to find your personal style.

☑ Use clothes as a way to express to the world who you are, not how you fit in.

☑ Boost your self-confidence with your personal style.

52

DEALING WITH THE PAST

LEARN TO OVERCOME YOUR STORY

To gain self-trust you must learn to get rid of any negative thoughts, give up any feeling of regret, and learn to overcome any bad experiences. We all have things in our past that best explains our current level of self-trust. What kind of stories do you have?

Write them down, and be honest. What do you have to deal with? Do you have any worries or regrets? Is there something you can learn from your past experiences? Get clarity on what moves you, and what could prevent your success. Put things into a new perspective.

Fight the monster under the bed. Constantly thinking of the past will not bring you anything, and will only lead to pessimism and sadness. Never regret anything and learn to overcome the past. Remove all negativity from your life. We all experience negative events and negative people, but we can make the choice to remove them as much as possible from our life.

Sometimes we are the cause of that negativity, but at other times it can be a particular situation, context, project or task. Or perhaps it is a person or multiple people. Articulate your worries and negative experiences, identify them and then remove those catalysts for negative thinking from your life. Think about the next months and ask yourself what you will achieve. Learn to find happiness in your life. What motivates you? What do you enjoy?

'Our key to transforming anything lies in our ability to reframe it.'

MARIANNE WILLIAMSON

Summary

☑ Thinking too much about bad experiences and bad stories, and constantly regretting your life, will not take you further ahead.

☑ Don't lose yourself in self-pity and grief.

☑ Learning to overcome all negativity is the best way forward. When you do that, you'll boost your self-trust significantly.

53

PLANNING FOR FAILURE

FAILURE IS NOT NECESSARILY BAD

This may sound a little counterintuitive, but failure can be an important part of success. You think failure has nothing to do with success? That is certainly false. There are many successful entrepreneurs who have had to go through failures and experience setbacks, even several times, before achieving success. Failures are a chance to learn and grow.

As an entrepreneur, you must face the possibility of failing. You cannot always rely on success. It is a good strategy to plan for failure, to be prepared for failure. Learn to live with risks, accept the status quo, and then learn to move on.

The thing is, no one ever can foresee what is coming so we are often surprised when we fail. And when we are not prepared for setbacks and failures, they hurt even more. When failure looks likely, recognise it for what it is—a setback, a fatal flaw— and then ask yourself what you can learn from it. And then stand up straight, take a deep breath and move forward.

A lot depends on how you deal with those moments. So plan for failure that might come, but don't let it surprise you. And when it happens, admit it wholeheartedly, embrace it, own it, think about what you can learn from it, write your story down, talk about it, and then move forward.

'Success is stumbling from failure to failure with no loss of enthusiasm.'

WINSTON CHURCHILL

Summary

☑ Failure is absolutely normal.

☑ Many people have failed before they have become successful.

☑ Be prepared for failure, and when it happens learn from it, grow in yourself and move on.

54

YOUR MINDSET DETERMINES YOUR SUCCESS

THE DIFFERENCE BETWEEN A FIXED AND A GROWTH MINDSET

Imagine this scenario: your boss gives you some work that is outside the scope of anything you have done before. What do you do? Do you think, oh boy, I have to prove myself now. I have to show how talented I really am. Or do you think, oh no, this exceeds my competence and skills. What if I fail? Or do you see the work as a challenge and chance to definitely learn something?

Your reaction will show your attitude and confirm your mindset. Your mindset has a profound impact on how you live and how happy you feel. Your mindset is developed over the course of your life as a result of your experiences.

According to Stanford psychologist Carol Dweck, there are two distinct types of mindset: fixed mindset and growth mindset.

People with a fixed mindset believe that their fundamental qualities (e.g. intelligence, talent) cannot be changed. They believe that their potential is determined by birth. A fixed mindset leads to less confidence, less motivation, and less curiosity. Such people give up more easily.

People with a growth mindset, however, believe that their fundamental qualities can be cultivated. They believe that through hard work and perseverance they can achieve more.

The problem with a fixed mindset is that the belief that we cannot change leads to a kind of victim mentality. And with a growth mindset, when we believe that we *can* change, we take responsibility for our lives. In other words, our mindset determines our success.

How do you feel about your abilities? What are your motivations? Do you give up easily? Are you a pessimist or an optimist?

Optimists have great self-trust. They are not smarter or more intelligent than others, but they do believe in themselves and in their abilities. The basic attitude of optimists is: 'I can do it.' Optimists never doubt their abilities. And if they don't reach their goals they don't feel like a loser. Optimists have positive visions and dreams. They concentrate on their strengths and not on their weaknesses.

The difference between optimists and pessimists:

- Optimists are solution-oriented; pessimists are problem-oriented.
- Optimists believe in themselves and their own abilities; pessimists do not.

- Optimists think, 'I can do it'; pessimists think, 'I cannot do it.'
- Optimists have positive self-talk; pessimists have negative self-talk.
- Optimists expect to win; pessimists expect to lose.

There are many benefits to having an optimistic mindset. Optimism even influences our health: it can lengthen our lives, and determine how we overcome life's obstacles. It can build resilience, and manage the risks of developing depression or other mental health issues. An optimistic mindset is contagious; such an attitude can spread to others like a positive contagion.

You probably think that optimistic thinking comes naturally to some people, but that's not so. It is a mindset that you can practise and cultivate. Optimism can be learned. It is like a muscle that you can build and strengthen. Learn to be an optimist and influence your self-trust, health and success.

'A pessimist sees the difficulty in every opportunity, an optimist sees the opportunity in every difficulty.'

WINSTON CHURCHILL

Summary

☑ Your mindset determines your success.

☑ A growth mindset is an advantage in life.

☑ Work on your mindset.

☑ Be an optimist in life and learn to see the positive side of things.

☑ You will strengthen your health by thinking optimistically, and increase your self-trust and success.

55

ACT NOW

DON'T WAIT FOR THE LIGHTS TO TURN GREEN

Success is often a question of making the right decisions. People are often afraid to act. They hesitate, believing that they will do something when the conditions and circumstances are right. This is like saying that when all the lights turn green they will leave the house and drive to work.

If you want to be successful, you should learn to forget such thinking. You cannot rely on the perfect circumstances. The conditions will never be perfect. If you procrastinate over minor details, you might never fulfil your dreams. There's no question that the hardest part of doing anything is making a start. It's much easier to succeed if you have a plan. Work out a great plan and follow through on it. Any task, no matter how big, can be made so much easier if you have a list of clear directions. Just don't wait until all the traffic lights turn to green before you commence. Start now. Create something. And keep working at it.

'Procrastination is the grave, in which opportunity is buried.'

ANONYMOUS

Summary

☑ We are often our own greatest hindrance to success by waiting too often for the best conditions and circumstances.

☑ By waiting, we miss opportunities and struggle to achieve success.

☑ Circumstances will never be perfect, so give up waiting and act now.

56

FOCUS AND VISUALISE YOUR SUCCESS

WHAT YOU ENVISION WILL HAPPEN

All top performers, no matter what their discipline, know the importance of picturing themselves succeeding in their minds, before success really comes. If you want to be successful, you have to visualise your success. You have to spend your time in thought, creating a detailed picture of your success. Visualise yourself sitting in a new office, doing new things with a new title and new responsibilities.

This is what we call daydreaming. Why not spend a few minutes every evening daydreaming right before you go to bed? When you can clearly and consistently see the future state you aspire to, you will be best prepared to achieve it. Learn from these examples:

- Boxing legend Muhammad Ali always found it important to see himself victorious long before the actual fight.
- Jim Carrey, as a struggling actor, used to picture himself being the greatest actor in the world.
- World champion golfer Jack Nicklaus said: 'I never hit a shot, not even in practice, without having a very sharp in-focus picture of it in my head.'

These people, among others, mastered the technique of positive visualisation, and openly described it as a success tactic. The advantages of such visualisation techniques:

- Leads to motivation
- Activates the creative subconscious to generate creative ideas
- Programs the brain to perceive and recognise the resources needed for success
- Activates the Law of Attraction for drawing the needed people into your life (see Key Quality 6 for further information)

By the way, the brain does not differentiate between a real memory and a visualised one. This means that when you imagine something vividly and with emotion, your mind records it as a real memory. The situation will become the same as something you have already experienced.

The problem in life is that we only see the obstacles that prevent us from achieving success, and far too often we allow these obstacles to become so big in our minds that they inhibit us from moving forward. This is why so many people settle for mediocrity.

Envision yourself successful like Muhammad Ali, Jim Carrey or Jack Nicklaus. What will it take and what sacrifices will you make?

Close your eyes right now and imagine how you can be successful. See it in vivid detail in front of you. Remember, the most important resource you can have for your business is focus. This is more important than money, time or the release of your next product.

Take a piece of paper and write down the following words: 'I make the commitment to earn _____ euros/pounds/dollars [*the actual sum of money you want to earn*] in the next twelve months.'

> 'Man is nothing other than what
> he makes out of himself.'

JEAN-PAUL SARTRE

Summary

☑ If you can't picture yourself in your own mind being successful and running a great business, chances are you will never succeed.

☑ Learn to have focus.

☑ Visualise, on a daily basis, your success until you notice desirable changes in your behaviour, confidence and skills.

KEY QUALITY 2: AUTHENTICITY/ CREDIBILITY/ TRUSTWORTHINESS

THE VALUE OF AUTHENTICITY, CREDIBILITY AND TRUSTWORTHINESS

We don't like or trust people who come across as phony and false. Thus, we avoid such people. We seek out friends and colleagues who are authentic. The more virtual our lives get, the more we hunger after something genuine. Customers don't want a product or a service; they want an experience ... an experience that is honest and transparent, more authentic.

Consumers today are no longer willing to accept inconsistencies between the image a brand projects and the reality of what it represents. A great majority of customers around the world expect brands to be honest and authentic. The question is no longer whether to be authentic; it has become a necessity to always be authentic.

Studies have even shown that honesty and authenticity are more important than product utility, brand appeal and brand popularity when it comes to driving consumer behaviour. Authenticity delivers high return on investment (ROI). Authenticity is really important, but what exactly do we mean by the term?

Authenticity

What is authenticity? Authenticity means staying true to who we are, what we do, and whom we serve. It is a measurement of the strength of our character. The Merriam-Webster dictionary defines authentic as 'true to one's own personality, spirit or character'.

In psychology, authenticity refers to self-knowledge and making decisions that are congruent with that self-knowledge. Seth Godin, bestselling author, entrepreneur and agent of change, says: 'Authenticity for me is doing what you promise, not 'being who you are'.'

Authentic people possess these qualities:

- Realistic perceptions of reality
- Knowledge of where they come from and who they are
- Acceptance of themselves and other people
- Thoughtfulness
- Ability to express their emotions freely and clearly
- Ability to choose a narrative that best suits their situation

- Willingness to learning from their mistakes
- Understanding of their motivations
- Avoid presenting themselves in a false way
- Avoid playing a role
- Avoid looking for other people's approval
- Consistency in word and deed
- Originality
- Avoid resting on their laurels

To establish your authenticity consider the following:

- Explore your autobiography
- Go on holiday with old friends
- Avoid comfort zones; step out of your routine
- Seek honest feedback from colleagues, friends and family
- Show your weaknesses
- Get to know other people better
- Care about the work others do
- Give people useful feedback
- Actively engage with your audience
- Be on hand to offer assistance
- Be responsive when people try to contact you
- Show the real you
- Remain true to yourself, your business and your core values
- Define the purpose behind your business
- Share your passions, mission and vision
- Be transparent and give evidence wherever you can
- Be honest and accountable for your mistakes
- Position yourself as an authority in your industry
- Be consistent in your efforts

Reasons why authenticity works:

- Builds identity and image
- Builds trust and influence
- Gives substance to business and products
- Tells people that what is on offer is of high quality
- Enables people to relate to your business
- Encourages engagement
- Elevates a business above the competition

Customers love authentic brands. Authentic brands don't try to be something they're not. Instead they recognise what they are, what they do best, and what customers value most about them. Some examples of authentic global brands:

- Google
- McDonalds
- Samsung
- Microsoft
- Apple
- Amazon
- Carrefour
- KFC

You don't need to be a great brand to be authentic. You need to know what you stand for and understand your customers, and utilise that knowledge in every customer interaction.

A good leader must also be credible, and be seen as trustworthy. If you're not credible, you won't be respected, and you won't achieve your potential as manager or leader.

Credibility

What is credibility? Credibility is not the same thing as being likeable. From the moment you start up a business, you are building your credibility. Credibility is your reputation, and it helps people decide if what you say has truth behind it. It takes time to build and it's formed by your communications with other people and the way you conduct yourself in business. Credibility and communication are closely linked. How you interact leads to credibility.

Credibility is like a linear scale on which others give you a rating. It is a perceived quality, one that people assign to you based on the interplay of certain elements. There are four elements of credibility:

1. Integrity: According to researchers Kouzes and Posner, the number one trait people are looking for in a leader is honesty. How to boost your credibility with regard to integrity:
   - Clarify your values, and examine your behaviour accordingly
   - Make a commitment to consistently tell the truth
   - Put emphasis on ethical behaviour
   - If you make a mistake be truthful about it
   - Give credit to colleagues and subordinates for their work
2. Competence: Experts enjoy a much higher degree of credibility than those who lack expertise. We rely more on people who can demonstrate expertise, which comes from a combination of a person's education and experience. How to boost your credibility with regard to competence:
   - Invest time in a better education if necessary
   - Obtain a licence to practise or a professional certification appropriate for your field

- Participate in meetings, ask probing questions and make insightful comments
- Attend conferences in your field
- Engage in continual learning

3. Sound judgement: A credible person can be counted on to analyse complex situations, ask intelligent questions, and make good decisions. A person who has sound judgement usually has cognitive and intuitive gifts as well. This person will take a big-picture rather than a myopic view and has a long-term rather than a short-term perspective. How to boost your credibility with regard to sound judgement:
   - Consider the impact of your decisions on other departments and groups
   - Ask others for input into your decisions
   - Avoid making judgements too quickly
   - Be willing to admit mistakes
   - Read good books and listen to tapes by management and relationship specialists
   - Stay current on the present trends within your industry and company

4. Relationship sensitivity (emotional intelligence and empathy): People with high credibility know how to ask questions about others' values and interests. They listen intently and with empathy, and have a high emotional intelligence. They can be trusted to listen to and to work in the best interests of others. How to boost your credibility with regard to be sensitive to relationships:
   - Be willing to learn from others, and from your own mistakes
   - Demonstrate concern for others' values, goals, interests and objectives
   - Learn to listen well

- Take time to build effective relationships with informal conversations
- Don't talk behind people's backs
- Be generous with credit to colleagues and subordinates
- Take time to understand other people's points of view

People will assign to you a certain degree of credibility based on how they rate you on the interaction of the following four elements of credibility: integrity, expertise, sound judgement, and relationship sensitivity.

Remember that your credibility is based on observed behaviour, not on your intentions. As an example of earned credibility, McDonalds has earned credibility with customers by revealing the ingredients of its burgers and fries.

Credibility is a package, which means that no single element alone described here will guarantee you high perceived credibility. The third important factor we should talk about now is trustworthiness.

Trustworthiness

What is trustworthiness? Trustworthiness means being reliable, keeping our promises, doing what we say we will do. Relationships are about trust. When we deal with another person, we often expect something. Basically, trust is a form of projected expectation. It is an assumption that a person is going to behave in an adequate way. We assume they will act in an honest, authentic and credible way. We rely on what the person promises and we insist on the person's transparency. And when we get to know the person better, we trust the person more. We develop a feeling of safety. We begin to trust. And finally, to us this person is trustworthy.

Trustworthiness decides whether people trust us or not. In business, the key to a strong reputation and to success is trustworthiness. Trustworthy people possess these qualities:

- Authenticity, credibility and transparency
- Grounding and principles
- Courage and the willingness to stand alone
- Openness and willingness to listen to others
- Sense of fairness; they will do what's right
- Directness and truthfulness
- Decisiveness
- Empathy and benevolence; they have heart
- Willingness to give up power
- Belief in the people they lead
- Humility as a leadership strength
- Competence and character
- Reliability
- Honesty

To establish your trustworthiness, consider doing the following:

- Be authentic
- Develop your credibility
- Show your integrity
- Clarify your intent
- Demonstrate your capabilities
- Deliver results
- Talk straight
- Demonstrate respect
- Admit mistakes

- Create transparency
- Show loyalty
- Help everyone win
- Provide regular feedback
- Improve yourself
- Confront reality
- Clarify expectations
- Share information
- Practise accountability
- Listen first
- Keep commitments
- Act consistently
- Extend trust

The first pillar of trust is ability. The second pillar of trust is integrity. The third pillar of trust is benevolence.

'If we can learn to trust one another more, we can have unprecedented human progress.'

FRANCES FREI

Summary

☑ The 2nd Key Quality of a Key Person of Trust is authenticity, credibility and trustworthiness.

☑ Authenticity and credibility are critical for success.

☑ Trustworthiness decides whether people will trust you or not, and trust is the key to success.

58

AUTHENTICITY IS A PARADOX

WE ALL WANT AUTHENTICITY BUT STRUGGLE OURSELVES

Authenticity has become the standard for leadership. But being authentic can take courage. Being authentic is making the choice to be true to your core values, and true to yourself. The problem that may arise is it can make you vulnerable, and vulnerability is often seen as weakness. However, it is no weakness. In fact, authenticity can be seen as strength because authenticity builds trust.

If you want to be seen as authentic, as a trustworthy person, you should be aware that there is nothing bad about being vulnerable. It shows that you're human. But none of us is perfect. We all make mistakes.

There is a paradox in authenticity. We all want others to be authentic, in everything, but we often struggle to be authentic ourselves. True influence and leadership aren't based on being different than you are. True influence and leadership are based on your authenticity and your willingness to develop your character. Authenticity requires a fine balance between tact and truth. Authenticity is a perception. It's about how others perceive us. Authenticity is a reflection of who we are. No one can look into the mirror and say: 'I am authentic.' That is not possible.

'Authenticity is a collection of choices that we have to make every day. It's about the choice to show up and be real. The choice to be honest. The choice to let our true selves be seen.'

BRENÉ BROWN

Summary

☑ Authenticity is about how others perceive you.

☑ Authenticity leads to trust and influence; it is a strength.

☑ Never be afraid to be authentic.

☑ Authenticity will increase your chances of success.

59

CREDIBILITY-KILLING BEHAVIOURS

UNDERMINING INTELLIGENCE AND PROFESSIONALISM

Through our behaviour, we often add to our burdens and cause stress in our lives. Credibility is quickly destroyed. We often act thoughtlessly, too spontaneously, and try to impress with false things. But it doesn't have to be that way. Here some examples of what you should avoid:

- Using negative self-talk; don't say things like: 'I am such an idiot'
- Criticising your own behaviour/judging yourself
- Regretting your deeds; never regret anything
- Compulsively apologising; apologies are not always necessary
- Blaming others and not feeling responsible

- Constantly seeking approval
- Smiling dishonestly, only smile when you are genuine
- Overusing flattery
- Failing to listen to what other people have to say
- Judging other people without really knowing them

'The more you are willing to accept responsibility for your actions, the more credibility you will have.'

BRIAN KOSLOW

Summary

☑ Credibility can be quickly destroyed.

☑ Avoid acting in a credibility-killing way.

GUIDE TO TRUSTWORTHY COMMUNICATION

WHEN YOU WANT TRUST, YOU SHOULD BE TRUSTWORTHY

There is no doubt that good communication is essential for any successful project. Trustworthy communication is one of the most important factors for success.

The lack of efficient communication will quickly hinder a positive working environment and prevent trustworthy relationships. Building trust in communication is considered an essential element in leadership and in business.

Here some suggestions for effective communication:

- Be open to others
- Be interested in others' problems and stories
- Learn to listen
- Be supportive
- Give others a fair chance
- Encourage and praise others
- Have patience with others
- Be honest, but always be fair
- Be transparent
- Be grateful
- Have kind words for others
- Create a positive atmosphere
- Have time for others

'Creating trust is paramount in communication.'

KARIN SEBELIN

Summary

☑ How you talk and interact helps to create trust and make you trustworthy.

☑ Learn to communicate in a trustworthy way.

KEY QUALITY 3: CHARACTER + ATTITUDE

ATTITUDE MAKES A HABIT AND HABIT MAKES CHARACTER

Let's clarify the difference between character and attitude. Attitude is the stance you take when you approach a given situation. Character, on the other hand, makes you do a particular thing even when the world is watching. We demonstrate character through having a strong will, and having certain values and principles, and by standing by our own opinion.

Character is what each person is within. Attitude can change according to the situation. Abraham Lincoln was a role model for character. His character is an inspiration for anyone seeking to become a better person. Abraham Lincoln said: 'Character is like a tree and reputation like a shadow. The shadow is what we think of it; the tree is the real thing.'

Many people believe their job is to manipulate this 'shadow' rather than tend to the health of the 'tree'. But in our world of transparency and democratised media, there can be no image management without behaviour management.

With regard to character and attitude, we can develop ourselves in one of four ways:

1. Build the right character with the right attitude (best case).
2. Build the right character with the wrong attitude.
3. Build the wrong character with the right attitude.
4. Build the wrong character with the wrong attitude (worst case).

To develop your character, begin by having a good attitude and cultivate good habits. Good habits lead to character; in fact they form your character. Character comes from doing things day by day, repeatedly.

'Character is habits visualised.'

KARIN SEBELIN

Summary

☑ The 3rd Key Quality of a Key Person of Trust is character and attitude.

☑ Learn to develop good character and attitude.

☑ If you have difficulty developing good character, start first with a good attitude and develop yourself further from there.

☑ Your mindset is formed by repeated habits.

IT'S ALL ABOUT PERCEPTION

DECIDE HOW YOU WANT TO BE PERCEIVED

Perception is everything. Many people are confident that they will leave the right impression, while others think it is too difficult to influence what others think about them. An important part of building our personality is to harness the power of perceptions. If other people's perceptions influence the success of our brand, we need to be purposeful about managing the perceptions we engender in others.

How others perceive us will have a significant impact on how they relate to and react to us. It may not always be easy managing other people's perceptions. We may have one view of ourselves while others have a very different view.

How we see ourselves is internal, or self-perception; how others see us is external perception. Problem is only, we filter the cues we get from others through our concept of self. We judge ourselves through our intentions, but we judge others by their actions.

Our concept of ourselves has been shaped in fundamental ways by our primary caregiver when we were infants. The way the caregiver responds to a child's first cries and gestures heavily influences how that child expects to be seen by others. 'Children behave in ways that perpetuate what they have experienced,' says Martha Farrell Erickson, senior fellow with the Children, Youth and Family Consortium at the University of Minnesota.

A positive self-perception is critical because our self-perception determines our self-confidence. But too often our self-perception is created by bad experiences, including repression.

The 'Johari window'[4] is a graphic illustration in psychology of the difference between self-perception and perception by others. The Johari window was developed by the American social psychologists Joseph Luft and Harry Ingham in 1955 (the scientists' first names served as namesake). This communication model is based on the theory that interpersonal communication gets better when self-perception and perception by others coincides. The model is primarily used in self-help groups and corporate settings as a heuristic exercise.

When using the Johari window, we distinguish between the section of the personality that is known to others and ourselves (e.g. our social interests), the section that we keep secret (e.g. our fears and doubts), and the section that is not known to us but is known by others. We tend to call that last section a 'blind spot'. These are the impressions we make on others but are not conscious of ourselves.

---

4 http://en.wikipedia.org/wiki/Image:Johari_Window.PNG.

There is also a fourth section, and that is the perception that is neither known to us nor to other people. This relates to our subconscious, which we signal subliminally but don't completely recognise. Here is an illustration of the Johari Window:

	Known to self	Not Known to Self
Known to Others	**Arena**	**Blind Spot**
Not Known to Others	**Façade**	**Unknown**

Through perception by others we can correct our self-image. When others hold a 'mirror' up to us and show us our false behaviour, we realise where we should change something. Feedback is a great way to communicate perception by others. Receiving feedback by others helps us understand where we have to change something.

With regard to perception, follow the advice of angel investor Judy Robinett: 'If three people tell you you're a horse, buy a saddle.' In other words, we should listen to what the outer world is telling us, because these people are probably right. Other people's feedback can help us get a good feeling for ourselves, and feelings create lasting perceptions. When you make a truly positive impact on another person, you leave them with a warm feeling, and strong feelings create lasting memories.

Maya Angelou said: 'I've learned that people will forget what you said, people will forget what you did, but people will never forget, how you made them feel.' When you affect people's behaviour by giving them a positive perception, you can impact your performance. Simply put, perception affects behaviour, which affects performance.

*'It isn't what they say about you,
it's what they whisper.'*

ERROL FLYNN

Summary

☑ Self-perception and perception by others are two different things.

☑ We see the world through our own eyes, and often have a different opinion and a different view of things than our counterparts.

☑ Use the perception of others and their feedback to correct your self-image.

☑ Aim for great feelings and lasting perceptions.

63

BODY LANGUAGE, OR MAKING FIRST IMPRESSIONS

WIN WITH BODY LANGUAGE

When it comes to first impressions—when we're deciding whether we like or dislike someone—body language is everything. Scientific studies confirm that body language is extremely important when we want to leave a good impression, form new relationships or maintain existing relationships.

The psychologist Albert Mehrabian, known best for his publications on the relative importance of verbal and nonverbal messages, postulated the 7-38-55 rule of communication. According to this rule, three elements are important for first impressions:

- Words are 7 percent of the message
- Tone of voice is 38 percent
- Body language is 55 percent

Understanding the science behind your message is an essential first step to building relationships of trust. There are several things you can do to harness the power of body language and build better relationships of trust:

- Make eye contact: Numerous studies have shown that the more people look each other in the eyes, the more they like each other. Research teaches us that we maintain eye contact 40-60 percent of the time we're talking to someone; however, when we become the listener we maintain eye contact with the speaker 80 percent of the time. Ideal eye contact lasts approximately 7–10 seconds in a one-on-one conversation. If you look away too soon you risk implying that you're untrustworthy. Excessive blinking is suspicious. Adults normally blink 15–20 times per minute, but under pressure this rate increases.
- Mirror behaviours: Imitating others' behaviours, including body language, will convey that you are on the same page and creates feelings of empathy and trust. You can create a connection and gain trust with another person intentionally by simply mirroring their body language. If they're leaning forward, you lean forward. If they're gesturing with their hands, you gesture with your hands. But don't exaggerate these behaviours or people will get angry.
- Smile more often: The most important and easiest way to create trust is by smiling at someone. Learn to smile spontaneously and you will win hearts.

- Touch: Touching someone casually can create a subconscious bond and warm the other person's heart. Make sure it's really from your heart or it will seem insincere. You should know where to touch. Touching on the hand, forearm or wrist is acceptable.

*'Personality is an unbroken series
of successful gestures.'*

F SCOTT FITZGERALD

Summary

- ☑ A first impression can determine whether or not you have others' trust.

- ☑ When people see you as interested and warm, and recognise a convincing body language, you truly will make an impact.

- ☑ Start today and practise the power of body language with everyone you meet and you will watch the positive energy start flowing in your direction.

- ☑ The ability to attract other people gives you a real chance of success.

FOCUS ON THE PERSONALITY FACTOR

GIVING YOUR BUSINESS A FACE

The age of the faceless company is over. In the new business era of the 21st century, great brands must have a dynamic personality in order to attract attention. Make your personality stand out in every aspect of your brand-building process. Present yourself in a unique way. People aren't looking for another cookie-cutter company that has the same offers as everyone else. They are looking for a new experience tailored to their needs, and they want genuine personal interaction.

It's a question of how you want to be perceived:

- Personable and friendly
- Corporate and professional

- Spontaneous and energetic
- Classical and traditional
- Serious
- Funny
- Exclusive
- Established
- Accessible to all
- Tech savvy

Let your brand personality shine, and be consistent with that brand personality across all points of contact. The personality factor is the secret weapon in personal branding; your individual character and personality can make a difference. How can you use this to create success? Here are some suggestions:

- Be unique
- Show your personality
- Decide how you want to be seen by others
- Decide how you want others to describe you
- Show your face in public, or in videos; people want to see people
- Avoid trying to be perfect
- Be authentic
- Be yourself
- Have a strong attitude
- Have an opinion
- Take a position
- Accept feedback and criticism
- Stand by your personality quirks
- Show your humanity
- Show your vulnerability

- Show empathy
- Show that you have heart
- Act professionally at all times
- Have good manners
- Know what you want from life

'Personality is only ripe, when a man has made the truth his own.'

SØREN KIERKEGAARD

Summary

☑ Boost your success with the personality factor.

☑ Show yourself, don't be a faceless company.

☑ Have an opinion and stand by it.

☑ Build an effective brand personality.

☑ Stand out by letting your personality shine.

PERSONALITY VERSUS CHARACTER

PERSONALITY AND CHARACTER ARE NOT THE SAME THING

As a leader, it is important for you to understand the difference between personality and character. What is personality? Personality refers to your basic nature; how you were when you were born. In life there are extroverted and introverted people. Some are even-tempered while others are hotheaded. Your personality consists of the things you inherited genetically.

What is character? Character refers to how you choose to use your inheritance to make your way in the world. Your character is built over time. It shows in the decisions you make, and it comes from living, learning and making mistakes.

There will be many situations in your life where your character is tested, where you have to prove yourself. In a crisis, when there are problems or temptations you will be tested and your true character revealed.

'When you choose your friends, don't be short-changed by choosing personality over character.'

W SOMERSET MAUGHAM

Summary

☑ With personality, you will get through the door, but character will ensure you stay there.

BUILD CHARACTER

IT IS NEVER TOO LATE

The person with a wise attitude understands that the problem of trust is ultimately a problem of behaviour. How you see yourself reflects how others see you. Your self-image is responsible for the construction of your mind.

Attitude leads to trust, and it is never too late to change your attitude. However, building a strong character is not easy. It takes self-awareness, humility, companionship, love and honesty.

If you want to lead a trustworthy life and enjoy success, you need to build a sustainable moral foundation that is rooted in solid character. Whatever your education, experience or age, building character is a lifelong process of learning. It is an evolution that involves awareness, attentive leadership and an ongoing commitment to 'grow' your good character and attitude.

Here are some suggestions for building good character:

- Define your values: Good character is built on personal beliefs and values, such as honesty and loyalty. Having good character means not jeopardising these values and standing firm by them.
- Think big: If you want to do something, do it. If you can dream it, do it. Stay motivated.
- Set yourself goals: Lead by example and aim at targets. Go above the norm.
- Take risk: Go out of your comfort zone, and learn to handle shortcomings and mistakes. Face challenges and learn to develop self-trust.
- Surround yourself with people of high character: Look for people you respect, who possess values and character traits that resonate with you. Learn from these people and enjoy being in their company.
- Work hard on yourself: Develop yourself further and be willing to learn. Building good character does not happen overnight.
- Be grateful for life: On the journey to build a strong character there will be ups and downs. Life is not always easy. Be grateful for what you have and be happy.
- Be open-minded and approachable: Be open to and interested in the outer world. Be receptive to people, be approachable. Character comes from being curious, and showing an interest.
- Lose amiably and fairly: Learn to lose and fail with a smile. Don't take failure personally. A person of character is a gentleman or a lady with style. Learn from setbacks and see them as new motivation.
- Learn to trust yourself: Concentrate on your strengths. Be confident in yourself and your own potential. Develop self-trust and courage.

- Remember successful moments: Enjoy wonderful moments in your life. These moments define your character. Situations, when you were in a challenging position and you successfully mastered it. Cherish these moments.
- Walk the walk: Your words should match your actions. Say what you mean, mean what you say, and also do what you say you will do. Living a life of integrity is the key to success. How can people trust you if you break your word?
- Be empathic and polite: People of high character demonstrate empathy and understanding for others. They are courteous and kind to other people. They support others without expecting anything in return.

'Character cannot be developed in ease and quiet. Only through experience of trial and suffering can the soul be strengthened, vision cleared, ambition inspired, and success achieved.'

HELEN KELLER

Summary

☑ Building, maintaining, and strengthening strong character takes will and time.

☑ Remain true to who you are, and remember that there might be people who look to you for inspiration.

KEY QUALITY 4: MAKE A DIFFERENCE/ KNOW YOUR UNIQUENESS + DISTINCTIVENESS

DIFFERENT IS NOT ENOUGH

In today's competitive world, it is not enough for you to present your products and services and share what you have to offer. This will not work. Learn to make a difference, and know your uniqueness and distinctiveness. Invest time and money in a thorough investigation into what differentiates your brand from the competitor's. Understanding the uniqueness of your brand and acting on this with a strong communication strategy is the key to creating a memorable and unique brand.

Be aware that being different is not enough. You must be unique. You must be distinctive. As a brand, you could very well be different, but only you can be yourself. Being unique is nothing more than a decision, nothing else. Decide for your uniqueness.

'Be proud of what makes you unique.'

KARIN SEBELIN

Summary

☑ The 4th Key Quality of a Key Person of Trust is making a difference, and knowing your uniqueness and distinctiveness.

☑ Focus on being different, and being unique and distinctive.

☑ Being different is not enough on its own.

68

THE IMPORTANCE OF BECOMING KNOWN

THE DIFFERENCE BETWEEN A COMMON AND A REMARKABLE BUSINESS

In today's fast-paced world, it is no longer about being a common business. When you want to stand out from the crowd—be different and remembered—you need to be creative and inventive. So many people present themselves without having a solid understanding of what is necessary for success. They act thoughtlessly, with only money and success in mind, and don't know what good relationships are all about.

There is a wonderful quote from John Quincy Adams that shows what is important: 'If your actions inspire others to dream more, learn more, do more and become more, you are a leader.' A great leader inspires others with their own actions.

Today it is about becoming known. And how do we become known? Through our actions we become known. By making a difference in people's lives, by offering support and reaching out to them, and by expressing our gratitude and appreciation. Here are some suggestions for showing your appreciation:

- Send a thank-you card if someone does something for you
- Send a thank-you card when you make a new contact
- Send a thank-you card after getting someone's business
- Send a Christmas card
- Send an anniversary card as a reminder of when you started doing business

These words by Robert Kiyosaki express these ideas so well: 'The richest people in the world look for and build networks, everyone else looks for work.'

Let me share a great experience with you. Today I received a thank-you card from a new LinkedIn contact thanking me for the contact. She wrote that she is very happy to have me in her network and is willing to introduce me to others in her network. Isn't that nice? It was a great surprise for me this morning.

I have learned that spontaneous actions are the best. People will remember them and will appreciate the connection even more.

'Anyone can make things that are beautiful; we need to make things that are remarkable.'

STEVE WYNN

Summary

- ☑ Don't be a common business, be a remarkable business.
- ☑ Become known through your actions.
- ☑ You will be remembered for your actions.

BE REMARKABLE

REMARKABILITY LIES IN THE EDGES

Everyone has the ability to become a remarkable person. Yes, even you. Being remarkable is not the same as being noticed. Running down the street naked means you will get noticed. It will not make you remarkable. Remarkability lies in the edges. Not everyone will appreciate your efforts to become remarkable, but your goal is not to please everyone. Instead, find your special target group, the people who love you.

Here are some suggestions for becoming a remarkable person:

- Overcome your fears: Face your fears and leave your comfort zone.
- Do what you love: Don't let the world dictate the terms of your life. Do what you love and enjoy happiness.
- Take risks: Be bold and never settle for less than you want.
- Listen to what others have to say: Learn to listen, and show your heart and your empathy.

- Expose yourself to a wide variety of topics: Learn something new every day (e.g. learn new languages, read good books).
- Find solutions for problems: Use your skills to solve problems and help others.
- Share your experiences and stories: Tell good stories, bad stories and be vulnerable.
- Impress with intelligence, wit and humour: Show others your sense of humour. Share your intelligence.
- Be open-minded: Show an interest in others. Talk to strangers.
- Help others: You don't have to change the world; one person's life is enough.
- Be honest: Stand by your words, and show your character. Never lie.
- Be yourself: Realise the potential inside yourself. You are remarkable the way you are.

'Don't live down to expectations. Go out there and do something remarkable.'

WENDY WASSERSTEIN

Summary

☑ Learn to be remarkable.

☑ Don't try to please everyone.

PREEMINENCE: HOLDING THE NUMBER ONE POSITION

PREEMINENCE MEANS CREATING IMPACT

The Strategy of Preeminence should become the underpinning of your business culture, hiring, marketing, and client interaction. Everything should flow from this powerful belief system and business view. Jay Abraham is world renowned for his Strategy of Preeminence, which is both a strategic philosophy, and a philosophical strategy for operating a preeminent business.

What is preeminence? The word preeminence is derived from the Greek word *proteuo*, which means 'to be first in rank or influence'. It comes from the word *protos*, which means 'foremost in time, order, or importance'. Think of the word prototype, which means 'the first type or model of something'. Preeminence is the idea of being first, or holding the number one position in the order of things.

The Strategy of Preeminence starts with overthinking the way you deal with your relationships, the way you have operated your business, and the way you have looked at your goal and purpose. Preeminence requires you to create impact in everything you do.

There are many ways to create impact. Richard Wiseman, a British psychologist, suggests fifteen ways to create a positive impact in the presence of others:

1. Treat every person as important.
2. Shake hands firmly and say positive things while doing so.
3. Keep your body language open.
4. Stand tall.
5. When speaking to a group, speak conversationally (don't read from a script).
6. Learn to remember people's names and use them in conversation.
7. Look people in the eyes.
8. Compliment people sincerely.
9. Acknowledge other people's strengths and accomplishments.
10. Use pauses while speaking and learn to emphasise important words.
11. Take care of your outer appearance.
12. Smile more often.
13. Listen to people's emotions and respond to them.
14. Use positive body language, make eye contact and move around while you speak.
15. Be genuinely interested in those around you.

'In all thy work keep to thyself the preeminence;
leave not a stain in thine honour.'

BIBLE APOCRYPHA

Summary

☑ Learn to become preeminent in the minds of your target audience.

☑ Begin by making an impact.

71

KNOW THYSELF

DEVELOP AN AWARENESS

Above the ancient Greek temple in Delphi is an inscription that reads: 'Know thyself and thou shalt know the universe and God'. Self-knowledge is very important. Only when you become truly aware of who you are and what you want from life will you find fulfilment. The British author Aldous Huxley wrote: 'Knowing who in fact we are results in Good Being, and Good Being results in the most appropriate kind of good doing.'

If you want to achieve a sense of purpose in life or at work, it is critical that you know yourself. Begin by asking yourself a few questions:

- Who am I in life and work?
- What do I want from life?
- What do I love?
- What are my dreams?

- What are my hopes?
- What are my goals?

By asking these questions you are making a commitment to develop, and to define your calling and your personal purpose. That's when you will really begin to know yourself.

'To know thyself is the beginning of wisdom.'

SOCRATES

Summary

☑ The key way to find your purpose is to first know yourself.

FIND YOUR PURPOSE

DISCOVER WHY YOU WERE BORN

What is your purpose? Why do you work? Ever thought about it? Purpose is what gives meaning to your life. What is the purpose of life in general? Some say that our purpose is to find happiness; however, trying to find or seek happiness is not a strategy.

Victor E Frankl, professor of neurology and psychiatry at the University of Vienna Medical School, held professorships at Harvard, Stanford, Dallas and Pittsburgh, and was a distinguished professor of logotherapy at the US International University in San Diego, California. He was a survivor of Auschwitz and other Nazi concentration camps, and wrote the book *Man's Search for Meaning*. In his book he writes: 'Don't aim at success—the more you aim at it and make it a target, the more you are going to miss it. For success, like happiness, cannot be pursued; it must ensue, and it only does as the unintended side-effect of one's dedication to cause greater than oneself or as the by-product of one's surrender to a person other than oneself ... Happiness must happen, and the same holds for success: you have to let it happen by not caring about it.'

When he was in the concentration camps, Frankl realised that the people who were most likely to survive where those who had a task waiting for them to fulfil. Frankl's own deep desire to write his manuscript and have it published helped him survive the rigours of the camps.

When you know your *why*, life will gain meaning, but you should never search for an abstract meaning of life. Frankl also wrote: 'Ultimately, man should not ask what the meaning of his life is, but rather he must recognise that it is he who is asked. In a word, each man is questioned by life, and he can only answer to life by answering for his own life; to life he can only respond by being responsible.'

A sense of responsibility is the very essence of human existence. We are all responsible for our own lives. We are responsible for our own happiness.

'The two greatest days in your life are the day you are born and the day you discover why.'

MARK TWAIN

Summary

☑ Never seek happiness or success; rather, let both happen.

☑ Find meaning and purpose in your life.

☑ Take responsibility for your own life.

73

CRAFT AN EFFECTIVE PURPOSE STATEMENT

DON'T JUMP ON THE CHANGE-THE-WORLD BANDWAGON

There are many companies that confuse purpose programs with corporate responsibility. Be aware that your company's purpose is not to save the world. Your company's brand purpose statement should not be about a promise that your products will raise the quality of life for all people, or for the whole world. Such promises are unrealistic. Don't jump on the change-the-world bandwagon. Instead, define a clear, effective purpose that makes sense.

Your company's purpose is its reason for existing. So why do you exist? Why does your company, your business, exist? Why do you do what you do? Your purpose statement should be the driving force behind all your actions, and the driving force for all decision-making.

If you want to define and implement a meaningful and effective purpose program, there are two critical requirements to be aware of. First, you must leverage the whole intellectual power of your organisation to generate a distinctive and actionable idea of what your purpose should be. Second, you should become a leader with the personal will, courage and compassion to take responsibility and actively model the vision expressed in the purpose statement, and use this to motivate your employees.

'A noble purpose inspires sacrifice, stimulates innovation and encourages perseverance.'

GARY HAMEL

Summary

☑ Purpose is not to be confused with corporate responsibility programs, through which companies fund education, research and sustainability, or support social issues.

☑ If you want to support social issues and charities, do it in a separate campaign.

☑ Develop and implement a meaningful and effective purpose program that makes sense.

74

THE JAPANESE CONCEPT OF IKIGAI

THE SECRET TO A LONG, HAPPY AND MEANINGFUL LIFE

Why do you wake up every day? What's your reason for getting up in the morning? If you have problems answering this question and would rather crawl back into bed, you could learn something about the Japanese concept of *ikigai*.

What is *ikigai*? It's a combination of the words *ikiru*, meaning 'to live' and *kai*, meaning 'the realisation of what one hopes for'. Together these words make the concept of 'a reason to live' or the idea of having a purpose in life. *Ikigai* covers four sectors:

1. What you love
2. What the world needs

3. What you can be paid for
4. What you are good at

With this knowledge you can find:

1. Your mission
2. Your vocation
3. Your profession
4. Your passion

Ikigai can lead to a better life, because you will have something to live for. For a good example of practised *ikigai* we can look at Okinawa, an island at the southernmost prefecture of Japan. This island has an unusually large population of centenarians. The concept of *ikigai* pervades the life of these islanders. Okinawans enjoy a particular diet and the support of friends, or *moai*. *Ikigai* is helping these people live longer as it gives them a purpose.

'Happy are those, whose purpose has found them.'

ANONYMOUS

Summary

☑ The Japanese concept of *ikigai* can lead you to a better life because you will have a purpose.

FIND YOUR EXPERT TOPIC

THE TOPIC THAT MAKES YOU AN EXPERT

Even if you have identified your expert topic this chapter should be of interest to you. When you are able to clearly identify your expert topic, you have set the foundation for a happy expert biography. It is worth investing some time in thinking about your expert topic. Successful experts have clarity, know what they stand for, and practise continuity in their field, which is not to say that they refrain from developing themselves further.

To find your own expert topic, start by thinking of your meta topic (your all-embracing topic). For example, you might want to know how to build an online business. If so, you need to come up with your expert topic, which could be online marketing.

Knowing what your basic topic is may not be easy. You might need to step back from the overall picture to identify it. Tip: it will be easier to detect your basic topic if you differentiate your central expert topic (meta topic) from the subsequent customer approach. You are not looking at your product title at this point.

Many people don't know immediately what they should put forward. There are often many possibilities. There are two options:

1. If you have started your career, systematically come up with topics that interest you. Compile a shortlist with ten possible topics, and then reduce these ten to three favourites. Consider what your strongest topic will be over the next few years.
2. If you are self-employed, systematically compile your topic fields, and throw out any that don't interest you. Reduce the rest to three favourites. Look for a strong topic that is related to these favourites, something that excites you professionally. Alternatively, you could combine an old and new topic.

It's important to note that you should only allow new things on board when old things are kicked out. In other words: 'Young rabbits can collect what they like. Old rabbits already have a collection.'

In both cases, deciding on one topic always means not to many others. It can be helpful to let the process itself find your topic for you. As life changes, it is often good to wait to see what life will bring.

Your expert topic is more than an experience. Someone who has learned to brush their own teeth is not necessarily a tooth-brushing expert. It is critical to consider what you have really mastered. Where are you able to lead others in a particular topic? To be an expert you need a knowledge advantage, and this can come from several things:

- Education
- Self-education
- Practical experience
- Biographically learning (own concern)
- Creation of something new; a new framework

This checklist should help you find your topic:

- Topic entry: Is there a special event, role model or book that makes you realise what your topic is?
- Certificates, special skills, and competencies: Do you have special/meta competencies, expertise or social skills?
- Expert status: Do other people already consider you an expert?
- Previous successes: What previous successes have you achieved?
- Special features in biography: What is different about you?
- Special identity: Is there something that makes you special, e.g. another nationality?
- Position that repels you: What is it that you don't want?
- Special relevance/concern: What topic makes your heart beat?
- Strong audience demand: Did you stumble upon a need that you do not understand, why no one has given a good answer here so far?

Whatever topic you choose is your business model. If you want to be successful with your topic, you should be aware of two things. First, the topic should be something that fascinates you (*heart*). Second, the topic should be something that others will jump onto (*taxi*). In these examples, *heart* stands for passion, *taxi* for demand. *Heart* alone will not suffice; you also need enough *taxi*.

*'Never become so much of an expert that
you stop gaining expertise. View life as
a continuous learning experience.'*

DENIS WAITLEY

Summary

☑ Your expert topic is the central foundation of your expert biography.

☑ Invest some time in finding your expert topic; it will pay off.

☑ First find your meta topic and then develop your expert topic.

KNOW YOUR CUSTOMERS' PROBLEMS

HOW WELL DO YOU KNOW YOUR CUSTOMERS?

Selling is about solving customers' problems. The real art in business is to find out what people's problems are. If you can solve a problem and use that as your final positioning, you will increase your chances of success. Customer problems are your opportunities for success. Don't ignore your customers' headaches.

Your customers want someone who understands their interests, difficulties and goals. There is a saying: 'People don't care how much you know until they see how much you care.' Forget about selling and think about how you can help solve people's problems.

How can you find out what people's problems are? That's easy. You just have to ask. Conduct surveys and hold interviews and ask people questions like: What are the biggest challenges you have to face today? What are the biggest challenges in growing your business?

The more you learn about your customers and their problems, the better you will understand how to make an impact in their lives. When you speak in your customers' language and show empathy, your relationships go to a higher level. You will create trust.

After identifying your customers' problems, learn to word the benefit of your offer as precisely as possible. Figure out what you offer that no one else is offering. Focus on the qualities and benefits that make your brand unique. Think about how to provide value that improves your customers' lives.

Be relevant. Relevance begins when someone believes that you understand and care about what's important to them. Your relevance to your clients or customers is determined not only by your products or services, but also by the efficient way you can solve their problems and meet their needs. Building relevance is a skill that could be called thinking in reverse. To do that, you must move out of your world into your customers' world.

'If you don't stay relevant, you will be relegated.'

BERNARD KELVIN CLIVE

Summary

☑ Know and understand your customers' problems and your benefit to them.

☑ Write down your customers' problems.

☑ Build your offer and message on your customers' perceptions, preferences, dreams, values and lifestyle.

☑ Word the benefit of your offer as precisely as possible.

☑ Be relevant.

WHAT YOU BRING TO THE TABLE

KNOW YOUR STRENGTHS, WEAKNESSES, VALUES AND GOALS

Before you learn to differentiate yourself from the competition, or learn about your unique selling proposition (USP), we should talk about strengths, weaknesses, values and goals. A good USP starts with an awareness of your strengths, weaknesses and values, and also your goals. The key is to learn something about yourself, specifically, what you bring to the table.

What are the three words that describe you best? When you've thought of these, follow up with these questions:

1. Where are my strengths? What am I good at? When you know the answers to these two questions you can adapt your business model and specialise.
2. What are my weaknesses? What are my blind spots? Where are my problems?
3. What are my values? What values are most important to me? What are my moral limits? What is important to me when interacting with other people? Knowing your values and using them is important. Learn to prioritise your top five values.
4. What are my goals? Reflect on what you want to achieve, and then commit to it.

Use the SMART[5] acronym to set goals and stick to them. Then you can plan the steps you need to take to realise your goals. SMART stands for:

- Specific: simple, sensitive, significant
- Measurable: meaningful, motivating
- Achievable: agreed, attainable
- Relevant: reasonable, realistic and resourced, results-based
- Time-bound: time-based, time limited, time/cost limited, timely, time-sensitive

Set SMART goals that motivate you, and write them down to make them feel more tangible. Ask yourself the following questions:

---

5 The acronym is commonly attributed to Peter Drucker's idea of management by objectives, and was first used in the November 1981 issue of *Management Review* by George T Doran. Professor Robert S Rubin (Saint Louis University) wrote about SMART in an article for The Society for Industrial and Organisational Psychology.

- Specific: What do I want to accomplish? Why is this goal so important? Who is involved? What kind of resources or limits are involved?
- Measurable: How much? How many? How will I know when it is accomplished?
- Achievable: How can I accomplish this goal? How realistic is this goal?
- Relevant: Does this seem worthwhile? Is it the right time? How does this relate to my other efforts or needs? Am I the right person to reach this goal? Is this applicable in the current environment?
- Time-bound: When? What can I do today? What can I do six weeks from now? What can I do six months from now?

Further tips for setting goals:

- See each goal as positive statement
- Be precise
- Set priorities
- Write down your goals
- Keep operational goals small
- Set performance goals, not outcome goals
- Set realistic goals

'Practice self-awareness. Once we know where our strengths, values and goals are, we are able to more easily embody the philosophy and leadership of our own uniqueness.'

KARIN SEBELIN

Summary

☑ Learning something about your strengths, weaknesses, values and goals is a critical process before defining your unique selling proposition (USP).

☑ Once you know your strengths, weaknesses and values, and what your goals are, you can differentiate yourself from the competition.

☑ SMART is an effective tool that provides the clarity, focus and motivation, all needed to achieve your goals.

☑ The key to success is to find awareness.

☑ You should know what you bring to the table.

WHAT IS YOUR SECRET SAUCE?

EVERY FOUNDER NEEDS A SECRET SAUCE

To be successful on the market, as founder you need a 'secret sauce'. These special ingredients will make your recipe—your product or service—unique and give your business a decisive competitive edge. Every founder needs such a sauce, for businesses are unknown at the beginning, as are their products. Potential customers are sceptical and hold themselves back from purchase.

A secret sauce should deliver considerable advantages towards, what the customer already knows. Such a sauce should not be missing in a pitch. With the help of such a sauce you can develop a product that is unique and remarkable.

Marketing expert Seth Godin says, 'You're either remarkable or you're invisible. Make a choice.' The ideal scenario is that your product will become the bill of lading among its potential customers, which means free marketing for the founders.

As an example, founders of Airbnb detected the secret sauce for their start-up by chance. They did not have much money, and during a conference in their town they rented three air mattresses for sleeping. That made them realise that travellers would be willing to spend the night in private accommodation. They also found out that house owners liked to earn something by renting unoccupied rooms to strangers. Since then, the company has mediated more than a hundred million overnight stays.

This concept of a secret sauce comes from the United States, with Colonel Harland Sanders telling us all about his delicious secret spice mix that, since 1940, led to the success of Kentucky Fried Chicken.

A secret sauce is characterised by three main traits: it is new in its field (no competitor has anything comparable), it gives a start-up a clear competitive edge, and it is not reproducible (at least not too fast).

Warning: offering something five percent cheaper is not a secret sauce. It's not a remarkable or unique trait. To be effective, a secret sauce needs some creativity. Fill in the blanks and create your own secret sauce:

1. We were the first to recognise that _____.
2. Consequently, we developed _____
    [solution] with _____ [secret sauce].
3. By doing that, our customers now receive _____
    [customer advantage] that no one else offers.

'The ultimate competitive advantage is having a unique secret sauce.'

KARIN SEBELIN

☑ Define your secret sauce for your business to attract prospects and thrill customers.

Summary

79

THE DIFFERENCE: POSITIONING AND UNIQUE SELLING PROPOSITION (USP)

YOU CAN'T BE EVERYTHING TO EVERYONE

The foundation of a strong brand is a great positioning and having a great unique selling proposition (USP). What is the difference between positioning and USP? Positioning and USP are similar, but they have some key differences: Positioning is based on an audience's perceptions. It will make sure you are seen, thought about, accepted and remembered. This marketing tactic focuses on creating a perception about your brand, product or service in your potential customers' minds.

A USP is based on the existing attributes of your product and services. A USP is tied to features and benefits, whereas positioning is much closer to branding.

Why is positioning so important?

Your audience could well be experiencing information overload, or content shock, because of the sheer volume of marketing and advertising messages they are bombarded with nowadays. The brain develops a kind of 'banner blindness' as a reaction to this. Content marketers need to use positioning to get in front of the audience.

I once had a client who asked me, 'Why should I position myself? I am what I am. I present myself the way I am, and why should I change that?'

To be clear, positioning yourself is *not* about changing your authentic attitude. It does not imply that you are something you are not. Authenticity is always important, and you should not play a role simply to reach people. But if you want to reach the right people, and be successful, you will need to position yourself.

Positioning is something you never want to change once it's in place, so it's critical to make it something you can commit to long term.

'The essence of positioning is sacrifice. You must be willing to give up something, in order to establish that unique position.'

AL RIES, *POSITIONING: THE BATTLE FOR YOUR MIND*

Summary

☑ A strong brand needs a great positioning and a great unique selling proposition (USP); learn what the difference is.

DEVELOP YOUR UNIQUE SELLING PROPOSITION (USP)

ATTRACT THE RIGHT PEOPLE

Now we'll begin to develop your unique selling proposition (USP). Determine your target audience. The key is to get specific; you cannot be everything to everyone. You must find your special niche and your special target group. Three factors are decisive:

1. Your desire: Whom are you trying to reach? With whom do you want to work?
2. Your purchasing power: What target group has purchasing power for your offer?

3. Your effectiveness: Who is reacting to your offer? Who is responding to your message? (You can check this on fairs, Facebook ads, and more.)

Developing a USP that defines your company in the marketplace is an important part of creating pricing power and a business that customers will genuinely love. With a strong USP, you can stand apart from the competition and actively focus your energy on creating things that cater for your ideal group of customers. This means that you will attract the 'right' people. Seth Godin, marketing expert, says, 'Instead of working so hard to prove the sceptics wrong, it makes more sense to delight the true believers. They deserve it, after all, and they're the ones that are going to spread the word for you.'

Companies that don't choose a dominant niche will never dominate anything, and will therefore struggle. If you try to be all things to all people, you will never become anything to anyone. Who would you choose if you needed a heart surgery? Would you go to your general practitioner or a heart surgeon? That's a dramatic example, but the question illustrates the problem. The fear that new entrepreneurs often have is that they'll miss opportunities that fall outside their market if they concentrate only on a special niche. But there is no benefit to spreading yourself too thinly. In a world full of generalists, be a specialist. Here are some suggestions for achieving this:

- Tailor your mission and message to meet the market's exact needs
- Narrow your focus
- Identify the detailed behaviour and lifestyle of your consumers
- Find out what people's interests are and what their problems are
- Define your skills and your strengths
- Identify a field in which you are better than others

- Come up with something you're passionate about
- Ask friends what you are good at

For example, target groups can include college students studying abroad and single parents who work from home.

Develop a buyer persona. Paint a picture of your consumers and then learn how to create a brand identity they can understand and relate to. Demographics are crucial to your business. Define your target audience by asking questions: Who will benefit from my products or services? What age are my customers? What geographical area does my company cover?

Think about different factors that are relevant:

- Age
- Location
- Gender
- Occupation
- Education level
- Ethic background
- Income level
- Family status

Psychographics are also important (personal characteristics of a person):

- Personality
- Attitude
- Values
- Interests
- Behaviour
- Lifestyle

A buyer persona is a tool that will help you understand customers who share common characteristics. It can be used to develop marketing strategies and tactics that include messaging, content and offers. A buyer persona is built from the real words of real buyers and tells you what prospects are thinking and doing. When you know how to help buyers evaluate your approach on their own terms, you can build a bond of trust that your competitors can't match.

You should also check out your competition. Who exactly are they? What do they say about themselves? Do they claim to be cheaper, faster, number one? What is their target group? Who are their current customers? Avoid going after the same market. Don't be a copycat. Find a market that your competitors have overlooked.

Analyse your products and services. Create a list of features, and list the benefits they provide. Now make a list of people who have a need that your benefit fulfils. Reflect on how your products and services fit into your target group's personality and lifestyle. How and when will people use your products and services? What features will appeal most to people?

Finally, ask these questions: Are there enough people who fit into my criteria? Will my special target group profit from my products and services? Can people afford my products and services? Can I reach people with my message? Are people easily accessible?

Avoid wasting resources like time, money and energy contacting people who will never be a good fit and will never buy. Divide your marketing list into small categories that are effective and build results. Remember: Amateurs go wide; professionals go deep.

'A brand becomes stronger when you narrow the focus.'

AL RIES AND LAURA RIES, T*HE 22*
IMMUTABLE LAWS OF BRANDING

Summary

☑ A strong brand needs a great unique selling proposition (USP).

☑ Defining your target market is an important part of your brand-building process.

☑ Once you know who you are targeting it will be easier to figure out which media to use to reach them, and tailor marketing messages that will resonate with them.

☑ The key to success is to be specific and stand out from the crowd.

☑ You should differentiate yourself.

☑ You cannot be everything to everyone.

☑ You should find your niche.

☑ Think about who your audience is.

☑ Develop a buyer persona.

☑ Identify your top competitors.

☑ Analyse your products and services to find out whether they meet the needs of your target group.

☑ Learn to position yourself.

☑ Attract the right people and find your ideal customer.

TIPS FOR GOOD POSITIONING

POSITIONING SHAPES EVERY ASPECT OF MARKETING

Positioning is never an afterthought. It is an idea that should shape every aspect of your marketing strategy. Some tips for good positioning:

- Include the strengths and weaknesses of your competitors: Markets are not as responsive to advertising as they used to be. There are too many products, too many companies and too much marketing noise. To be successful in this over-communicated society, your company must create a position in the perception of your customers, one that not only integrates your own strengths and weaknesses, but also those of your competitors.

You will not win in marketing through the strengths and weaknesses of your own brand. Customers will always make their buying decisions by choosing between several brands.

- Communicate a position, and not the advantages or characteristics of a product: Successful marketers try to *position* a product in the brains of their customers rather than focusing on the advantages or characteristics. Most marketing programs, however, are built around the characteristics and advantages of a product. This creates a problem. If customers consider a characteristic extremely important the market leader can copy that immediately. But what a follower cannot copy is the leading position of that market leader.

You will never win against a market leader simply by being better. You will win by being different, by being first in a position, by setting yourself up as the leader in your particular area. That leadership position will be much more valuable than any high-priced marketing budget.

Ask yourself if you could own this position completely. To illustrate the importance of the first-mover advantage, management thinks in products, e.g. the first to introduce a mainframe on the market. Marketing, on the other hand, thinks in terms of customer perception, e.g. the first mainframe in customer perception.

If you want to be successful you should think like a marketer and concentrate on this first-mover advantage. The winner on the market is not the one with the best brand, but with the brand that holds the leading position in the heads of the customers.

- Public relations comes first, then advertising: PR is perfect for bringing new ideas and credible brands to the notice of customers. Steve Jobs was a master at this. He started with the iPod, then the iPhone and then the iPad. Social media is one of the best PR tools because PR works mainly by word-of-mouth and not the general media coverage. Social media is a perfect word-of-mouth tool.

- Never attack a market leader upfront: Companies often make the fundamental strategic mistake of attacking the market leader upfront. The example of Xerox speaks volumes. Despite the failure of RCA and General Electric with mainframes, Xerox made the same mistake and attacked IBM upfront with regard to computers with Xerox data systems. The business rule states: never attack a company upfront that has established a strong position. You can go around their position, or position yourself underneath or above, but never confront them head on.

- Note the importance of the name of a company and its product: Think globally. The name is the hook on which the brand is moored to the product ladder in the minds of the customers. With a weak name, even the best brand in the world has no chance of being anchored in the minds of the customers. Marketing nowadays is a global game. Choose a global name that consists of English words, or that works well in the English language. A good example is Matsushita Electric. The company later rebranded its name and became Panasonic.

- Accept that you cannot please everyone: Greed is a human emotion that often leads marketers to make the mistake of trying to please everyone. But a product that tries to appeal to everybody usually doesn't appeal to anybody. Brand stretching is the enemy of positioning. The more a company stretches its own product lines and services under its brand, the more difficult it will be to find a position for the brand in the minds of its customers.

- Think long term: To deal with change and define your core business, you need to think long term. Positioning is a cumulative concept that draws its advantage from the long-term effect of advertisement. Thinking long term is one of the most important principles of positioning. Ask yourself how viable your positioning will be over the next decade. Could there be industry development or shifts that could undermine this positioning?

- Keep your positioning statement simple: Ask yourself whether your positioning statement is simple enough to be summed up in a few words. It must be simple enough to telegraph its meaning and value to your potential customers in a second. Some excellent examples: 'Think different' (Apple). 'Think small' (Volkswagen Beetle). 'We try harder' (Avis).
- Respond to a need: Your positioning should respond to a need that a specific segment of customers in your industry craves. Will it fulfil a largely unmet need?
- Demand comes before niche: It's better to go into a field where there is an audience than into a field where no one is. Niche is not everything.

> *'In a competitive crowded world market, it's the well positioned brand that stands out.'*

BERNARD KELVIN CLIVE

Summary

☑ Defining your positioning is very important for your brand.

☑ Positioning should never be an afterthought.

☑ This idea should shape every aspect of your marketing strategy.

82

REACTION AND INITIATIVE BRANDS: WHICH ONE ARE YOU?

FORGET BEING NUMBER TWO AND TAKE THE LEAD

There are two kinds of brands in the world: reaction brands and initiative brands. It's important for you to learn the difference. Initiative brands are innovative, forge new paths, and do things because of their own internal restless passion for something. Reaction brands simply follow the lead of other companies' brands. As an example, take the iPad versus the original Surface tablet. The iPad was the initiative brand, developed as a new experience and a passion for restless dissatisfaction with the status quo. The Surface tablet was a reaction product designed to enter the tablet market.

Are you innovative? Do you tend to take the initiative? Or are you a reactive type? Forget being only number two. Take the initiative; take the lead.

'Lead from the front.'

AUDIE MURPHY

Summary

☑ There are two kinds of brands in the world: reaction brands and initiative brands.

☑ Forget being number two and take the lead.

☑ Be innovative; be an initiative brand.

HOW PEOPLE DECIDE WHO TO BUY FROM

INFLUENCING THE BUYING PROCESS

One of the challenges any business has had to face since the beginning of time is how to influence people to purchase their goods and services. Ultimately, the goal is to get a consumer to buy something that they need or want but don't have, or to get rid of something they have but don't need or want. If you want to get people to buy your products or services, you need to understand how people make buying decisions.

First, a quick look at history. Fifty years ago, demand, utility, quality and price were the decisive factors behind every purchase. It does not work like this anymore. The market is flooded with products and offers, and customers are increasingly assessing products according to criteria that have nothing to do with quality. The hard facts are often identical, or the quality is difficult for the customer to discern. As a result, many customers make their buying decisions based on quality surrogates, such as:

- Number of customers
- Usability
- External image
- Corporate design
- Name recognition
- Empathy
- Colour of the product
- Quality seals
- Internet presence
- Credentials
- Service

How can you influence the buying process? As a businessperson, you want to solve a problem for the customer. And people trust businesses that give them good information that allows them to make an informed buying decision. People do business with people they like and trust. Nowadays many online purchases start with a Google or Amazon search. People will look for tests that have been conducted on the product. They search for product reviews and recommendations. Positive experiences always win.

Prospective customers are going to make their buying decisions based on one or more of six methods:

1. Relationships: A good relationship with a seller can facilitate a buying decision. How we connect, we communicate and interact decides whether people trust us or not. Positive and strong relationships with other people can lead to positive experiences. By relationships, I don't mean 'collecting' contacts. Effective relationships are about

getting to know people better, being interested in them, having heart and showing empathy. Nurturing relationships is an important part in the trust-building process.

2. Competency: Being competent means having knowledge, intelligence and wisdom. Being an expert in the field. You know what you're talking about. Competency wins people. When you show competency in a presentation or meeting, you attract attention. You can persuade others.

   Competency is a significant factor in the buying process. And it's not only real competency that wins; even perceived competency can win. If you have a confident appearance, you attract attention. Even better, an increase in your perceived competency increases your real competency. So don't just focus on competency, but also make sure you have a good presentation, put on a good performance, and have a great personality.

3. Experience: This means several years' experience in business, and reaching a certain level of expertise. Expertise is always an advantage. People put more trust in businesses that have been on the market for a long time. But experience also means that, having gained wisdom through books and learning materials, you have formed your thought leadership.

4. Personality: As already stated, personality is very important. If you have a good self-image and outer appearance, your behaviour is good and you have self-confidence, you increase your chances of success with regard to the buying process.

5. + 6. Differentiation and price: These two go hand in hand. You might think it will benefit you to increase your prices, but that is a false assumption. High prices are not always good. On the contrary, business that try to compete on price often come over as cheap, with poor-quality products. Discounting does not create a good incentive to drive sales; the maths just does not work.

Never differentiate on price. Instead, differentiate on quality, service and market position. Be first on the market. Be the best. Be unique. Be the perfect choice. Your goal is to attract the clients you are perfect for and repel those that are not a good fit. Don't be afraid to push some people away. It's better to look for prospects that will become loyal clients.

'Influencing the buying process is one of the greatest skills you can have nowadays.'

KARIN SEBELIN

Summary

- ☑ Times have changed.
- ☑ Demand, utility, quality and price are not deciding factors anymore.
- ☑ Customers often decide via quality surrogates that have nothing to do with product quality.
- ☑ Learn to influence the way people buy from you.
- ☑ Invest time and money in good relationships, competency, experience, personality, differentiation and price.
- ☑ Try to influence the buying process.

DIFFERENTIATE YOURSELF TO BEAT YOUR COMPETITOR

NORMALLY THERE IS NO COMPETITION

Normally, you should never focus too much on the competition. Once you have found your unique selling proposition (USP), your niche and your target group there will be no competition. That's because you are unique. You are different from others. You have learned to stand out from the crowd. Nevertheless, it's always good to learn something about how to differentiate yourself from your competition. Here are a few tips:

- You are better than your competition: Your competitor cannot sell your products and services; only you can. Ask your customers more insightful questions. Offer better service. Shine through your personality and your service.

- Focus on the customer's solution: Forget about standard marketing materials. Reach into people's world and look at things through their perspective.
- Let the customer see solutions they didn't think were possible: Customers often come into the buying process with pre-determined expectations. Help people see what they did not expect.
- View your product or service as an investment: Your product is not just a service but also an investment. Don't simply sell your product; sell an investment, even for a lifetime. Concentrate on the future.
- Focus on the person who benefits from the purchase: Don't just focus on the decision maker. Making a purchase is not just about saying yes. Sometimes the decision maker won't profit directly from the purchase. Concentrate on the person who does benefit from the purchase.
- Avoid using comparisons: Don't use comparison charts and mention the competition. Søren Aabye Kierkegaard said: 'Comparing is the end of happiness and the beginning of dissatisfaction.' You are unique and special, and your products and services are, too.
- Demonstrate your competitive advantage: Go beyond declaring a competitive advantage. Demonstrate why and how you are different.

Remember, uniqueness knows no competition, successful organisations don't compete, and only losers have competition. The successful business will be the one that withdraws from the competition and keeps out completely. That's because competition is not a factor for success. Make the competition irrelevant by changing all rules of the market. Create a temporary monopoly with novel and clever concepts that you implement successfully.

Here I want to recommend the book *Blue Ocean Strategy: How to Create Uncontested Market Space and Make Competition Irrelevant* by Renée Mauborgne and W Chan Kim, professors of strategy at INSEAD. The Blue Ocean Strategy represents the simultaneous pursuit of high product differentiation and low cost, thereby making competition irrelevant. The authors say that the key to exceptional business success is to redefine the terms of competition and move into the 'blue ocean', where you have the water to yourself.

Successful companies pay little heed to matching or beating rivals, or carving out a favourable competitive position. Their aim is not to outperform the competition. Instead, they focus on innovating at value. The more that companies focus on coping with the competition, or striving to beat the competition, ironically the more they will look like the competition.

'If you're a true warrior, competition doesn't scare you. It makes you better.'

ANDREW WHITWORTH

Summary

☑ Normally you should see no competition.

☑ Learn to differentiate yourself from your competitors.

☑ Stop competing and start creating your own success.

☑ Value-innovate and let the competition worry about you.

85

DIVERSIFICATION IS NOT THE ANSWER

NEVER FOCUS ON TOO MANY PRODUCTS

There is a common corporate positioning theme called diversification, whereby companies want to become known and successful as diversified manufacturers of a wide range of great products. In fact, the two concepts—positioning and diversification—are poles apart. A strong position on the market is built on major achievements, not on broad product lines.

General Electric, for example, is not known as a diversified maker of industrial, transportation, chemical and appliance products. It is known as the world's largest electrical manufacturer. A company might be able to make more money by specialising on many products, by diversifying, but you need to think about whether this makes sense for you.

*'Your focus should be narrow; never
focus on having too many products.'*

KARIN SEBELIN

Summary

☑ Don't become involved in too many
product developments.

☑ To be successful in the long run, forget
about diversification; diversification
and positioning are poles apart.

86

THE ADVANTAGE OF UMBRELLA BRANDING

SALVATION FOR CREATIVE MULTIPRENEURS

Maybe you offer a variety of products and services and are not willing to part with some of these products and services. Maybe you know that you should position yourself better and part with superfluous things in order to become more attractive for your target group, but you don't want to dispense with some products. Maybe you know that you should part with some products, but you believe you will lose customers and suffer financial loss if you do. Or maybe you have fear giving up the false service. Or maybe you have so many talents and interests that you're afraid you will lose your creativity and are not willing to give up anything.

There are many different perspectives. We humans have learned to hold onto our possessions compulsively. Giving up something does not fit into our scheme of things. After all, we are hunters and collectors.

What can you do to avoid suffering from the negative consequences of this? This is where the concept of an 'umbrella brand', or family branding, comes into play. An umbrella brand represents salvation for creative multipreneurs. Under the roof of the umbrella brand you are able to reunite the individual groups and service packages you have built up. The advantage of an umbrella brand: umbrella branding represents a marketing practice that involves being able to sell multiple related products under a single brand name.

A brand may have ten product lines, but the trust on that brand leverages the attributes of all the ten product lines. A former 'vendor's tray' is herewith structured into a meaningful corporate structure and brand system. The aim of such a 'roof brand' is to achieve great reach and simultaneously achieve great acceptance in the target group. Another great advantage of this kind of marketing practice is that once a well-known brand wants to introduce another product, there are no additional costs required for brand creation. A new product launch becomes easier and cheaper because it can find available recognition and market setup. Some examples of classical roof brands:

- Beiersdorf (Nivea, Labello, Tesa, Eucerin)
- Apple (iPhone, iPad, iPod, Macbook)
- Ferrero (Duplo, Kinderschokolade, Hanuta)
- Virgin Group Ltd (Virgin has thirty-three branches that operate under the Virgin name)

*'Don't ever, ever devalue your product. Ever. It's
the worst thing anyone can do to hurt your brand.'*

KEVIN PLANK

Summary

☑ Normally you should not focus on having too many services and products.

☑ If you are a creative multipreneur and can manage several services and products effectively, you might find your salvation in umbrella branding.

87

KEY QUALITY 5: LEARN TO PRESENT/ PERFORM

OVERCOME YOUR FEARS

You need not become the next Steve Jobs in order to present yourself successfully. No matter if you're going to be a keynote speaker or you just want to nail your next presentation, you can become successful. Being able to lead a great presentation can boost your self-confidence enormously. When you grow in yourself you attract attention, and attracting attention can help your business. When you can reach your audience with words, body language and the right actions on stage, you are on the way to the next presentation.

Presenting yourself may not be easy, but doing nothing will not help you progress. Resting on your laurels will not lead to success. Some useful tips for preparing a great presentation:

1. Decide on the one memorable idea you want to leave with your audience.
2. Think of a compelling reason why people should care.
3. Note three messages to deliver to your audience.
4. Include a demonstration or video with your presentation.
5. Know thy enemy, be clear about what you are up against.
6. Simplify your presentation, which means moving away from death by PowerPoint bullet points.
7. Practise what you want to present.
8. Make eye contact with members of your audience.
9. Speak slowly.
10. Ignore the naysayers and focus on those you can engage with.
11. Accept and channel your nervousness into passion.
12. Thank your audience at the end of your presentation.

'Success is the presentation of our abilities.'

KARIN SEBELIN

Summary

☑ The 5th Key Quality of a Key Person of Trust is being able to present and perform.

☑ Nervousness is normal and you should learn to overcome your fears.

☑ Practise, practise, practise; no one is born a master.

LEARN TO STEAL THE SHOW

ALL THE WORLD'S A STAGE

'All the world's a stage,
And all the men and women merely players;
They have their exits and their entrances,
And one man in his time plays many parts ...'

WILLIAM SHAKESPEARE, *AS YOU LIKE IT*

There's no doubt that Shakespeare was right. Our lives are full of moments where we must perform, whether it's at a job interview, school, meeting, sales pitch, industry conference or on a stage. We must always perform. Each of those moments requires us to play our role, to manage our anxiety and our self-doubt.

Each interaction you have with other people is a kind of performance. No matter how clever you are or how good you are at what you do, you can still suffer from doubts, anxiety and nervousness. If you want to become successful, however, you should learn to perform, and master the art of good presentation.

Good performers have the ability to attract people. They have learned how to attract attention. For sure, not everyone is a natural comedian or is even a natural-born entertainer, but you don't need to be an entertainer to become a performer. Performance can also be about connecting to others. Here are a few tips for finding a foothold as a performer:

- Seek spotlight moments in your life when you have the opportunity to speak up and learn from them.
- Learn to accept yourself and become comfortable in your own body.
- Master the elements of writing and storytelling by learning to plot stories and develop speeches.
- Learn to act as if; act as if you were a master.
- Use improvisation when things go wrong (George Gershwin said: 'Life is lot like jazz. It's best when you improvise.').
- Seize chances and say yes when opportunities are offered.
- Step into new roles personally and professionally.
- Learn from setbacks.
- Don't put too much weight on perfection.
- Celebrate your successes.

Being nervous is normal. Learn to live with your fears. Here are the essential elements of a good performance:
- Find your own voice: Be authentic, don't play a role, examine your self-image and develop your unique voice further.

- Find the right role for every situation: When you are in a job interview you have one role; when you are in a meeting you have another.
- Tolerate your fears: Learn how to deal with them, with your inner critic and negative thoughts.
- Find motivation: Ask questions. What do I want? Why do I want it? What must I overcome?
- Be objective: Don't be blind; instead, be sure about where you want to go and what you want to accomplish.
- Always be prepared: Do your homework before any interviews or meetings.
- Develop a compelling presence: Good performers make an impact with their presence and personality.

The joy of being an entrepreneur is that at least it's you that writes the script. You are the star of your own soap opera. Ask yourself what kind of script you are writing. What things do you have to overcome? What does the challenge look like? What is standing in your way?

'Work is theatre and every business is a stage.'

B JOSEPH PINE II AND JAMES H GILMORE,
THE EXPERIENCE ECONOMY

Summary

- ☑ Do you have a performer's mindset?
- ☑ Learn to connect with, inspire and persuade your audience.
- ☑ Wow your audience, and win praise and plaudits every time.
- ☑ Seize the chance of performing or presenting.
- ☑ Learn to steal the show.

89

LEARN TO PRESENT YOUR PRODUCTS

INFORM OTHERS ABOUT YOUR WORK

Success does not come from something unknown. Only when you inform other people of your work will you become known. We live in an age of too much. Each of us is bombarded daily by over three thousand advertising messages. An average supermarket in a small town would be a kind of sensory overload for someone who blundered into it without prior experience. How should they navigate among the twenty thousand products? And each year new products are coming onto the market. The customer is in stress. That's why smart manufacturers provide information on the benefits of their products.

With the huge, constant flood of products, whoever wants to be successful on the market must understand this. They must clarify the range of services they offer in the best possible way. How can people know about them if they are not informed? What good are those products if nobody knows about them? What good is it if others sell themselves better?

Intelligent entrepreneurs draw attention to themselves. They know how to present their products. Apple is a good example. Apple is a great brand that knows how to sell. The company presents each new iPhone in a spectacular show. Many people clamour to see this presentation despite the many other good companies that offer comparable products. The presentation makes the difference.

Do you know the story of the chicken and the goose? This story shows the problem well. The chicken knows how to present its own product: the egg. It cackles loudly and convincingly when it produces the egg. The goose, however, does not make a great noise when it produces its eggs. Instead, it simply runs away. In the end, the chicken gets the attention and the goose does not.

Learn to present your products and your work and you will get more attention. Quality is not enough to be successful on the market. Attention is a scarce, precious commodity, and you will need to battle hard for it on a daily basis.

'Your number one thing is your product, and you should present it well.'

KARIN SEBELIN

Summary

☑ Only when you present your products and your work well will you become known and attract attention.

☑ Attention is a scarce and precious commodity.

KEY QUALITY 6: VISIBILITY/ ATTRACTIVENESS

DON'T HIDE YOUR LIGHT UNDER A BUSHEL

You will only have success after you become visible. After all, how can people get in touch with you if you are not visible? A profile will save you time. When you gain visibility in your industry, the right people will be able to find you. Don't chase people, opportunities or deals. Instead, curate a qualified profile and let opportunities come your way. But take note: only a high-quality profile will lead to quality clients, partners, suppliers, investors and further exposure.

People who rank highly in their industry don't hide their light under a bushel. They make sure the right people know what they are up to. Great leaders know how to be heard.

Learn to improve your profile online and offline. Create your own key stories and hooks that the media and your audience will love. Discover simple tactics that will help ensure that Google loves you. Be authentic and avoid shameless self-promotion.

When you are visible, you attract people, and attracting people to you will open up new networking and relationship opportunities. With the right body language, communication and actions you will be able to engage people. What you say and do, and how you present yourself all play important roles in attracting people and will lead to your success.

'The power of visibility and attractiveness
can never be underestimated.'

KARIN SEBELIN

Summary

☑ The 6th Key Quality of a Key Person of Trust is greater visibility and attractiveness.

☑ A KPT enjoys great visibility and attractiveness for contacts, fans, followers and prospects through their personality, leadership and presentation.

☑ A KPT can attract dream customers.

☑ The ability to attract followers and make contacts has to do with learning about relationships.

DEVELOP A VISUAL IDENTITY

YOUR WORK SHOULD REFLECT YOUR BRAND

Brand identity involves everything that represents how your brand is perceived, and your visual identity includes the visual components of that. What is visual identity and why is it so important? The way you present yourself visually to the outer world is more than just colours and design. It is about consistently presenting a visual identity that resonates with your audience.

Your visual identity reflects your company. Therefore, you should invest time, research and money to make sure it's represented accurately and positively, in line with your message. Your brand should be visible and reflected in everything your customer sees, reads and hears.

To create a great visual identity, ensure that your brand looks the same everywhere. Your logo will be seen almost everywhere, so you want to make sure you do it well. Use a brand style guide to create consistency with visuals (colours, logo, fonts, etc.). Using a brand style guide, you can ensure that your company image is always presented with the same colours, design elements, fonts, logo, and profile image.

The colours you choose should reflect the personality of your brand. Create a font that fits your brand personality. Choose images that address your audience and reflect your brand. A strong brand style guide that has visual-recognition value should include the following elements:

- Logo size and placement
- Colour palette
- Typography and fonts
- Iconography
- Photograph/image style
- Web elements

Use your visuals to steer emotions. With regard to your website, incorporate your voice, message and personality into the content. Your profiles on social media should be branded visually, too.

'It's a visual world and people respond to visuals.'

JOE SACCO

Summary

- ☑ Your brand should be visible and reflected in everything your customer sees.
- ☑ Develop a visual identity.
- ☑ Develop a brand style guide.

CREATE A BRAND LOGO AND A TAGLINE

THE VISUAL RECOGNITION OF YOUR PROMISE

Probably the most exciting part of the brand-building process is creating a brand logo and a tagline for your company. Why is a brand logo so important? Your logo will appear on everything that relates to your business. It is your identity, your calling card and a visual recognition of your promise to the world. Therefore, you should invest time and money into the process of developing your logo.

Try to create something exceptional. Hire a professional designer or creative agency to help you create a brand logo and tagline. Their knowledge and expertise will ensure that you get a high-quality product.

What is a tagline? You probably know Nike's slogan: 'Just do it.' This is a tagline. A tagline is a short phrase that captures a company's brand essence, personality and positioning, and distinguishes the company from its competitors. Taglines are meaningful and memorable, and require frequent and consistent use. They can also be protected and trademarked.

Branding expert and author Laura Ries says: 'Taglines can be cute, funny, flippant or irrelevant, but they generally have little to do with what makes a brand successful. Taglines are like the road sweepers at the end of a parade. They call attention to the fact that the commercial has come to an end. But they seldom position the brand.'

Nike's tagline doesn't tell you why you should use Nike's products. It acts as a brand trigger. When you hear and see Nike's tagline, you instantly associate the tagline with the brand.

'Logos and branding are so important. In a big part of the world, people cannot read French or English, but are great in remembering signs.'

KARL LAGERFELD

'A tagline is a slogan, clarifier, mantra, company statement, or guiding principle that describes, synopsises, or helps create an interest.'

DEBRA KOONTZ TRAVERSO, *OUTSMARTING GOLIATH*

Summary

☑ Invest time and money in developing a valuable brand logo and tagline.

☑ Make sure your tagline represents your brand essence.

THE ADVANTAGES
OF KEY VISUALS

A KEY VISUAL CAN BECOME
YOUR TRADEMARK

A key visual (image) can be any graphic, pictorial, colour, three-dimensional, visualised idea or figure that is closely linked with a brand. It can be used in every form of communication as a symbol for a brand. A key visual can become your trademark. It is the key image of a message that can stand for your product/s. A key visual is a successful sign of uniqueness, identity and quality. (As an interesting side note, key visuals are stored in the right-hand side of the brain, and brand names are stored in the left-hand side.)

You're probably aware of the famous stripes on the Adidas sport shoes, the Mercedes star, the Ferrari horse, the Milka chocolate cow, and the Swarovski swan. Key visuals stand for continuity and consistency; they often represent the key for brand awareness. Advantages of key visuals:

- Key visuals will help you to be identified in the minds of your target audience.
- Key visuals can increase the value of your positioning.
- Key visuals can become collectibles, with a corresponding increase in value.
- Key visuals can be used on all forms of communication, including business documents, price labels, product packages, offers and advertisements.

How do you find an appropriate key visual? Start by listing all the special strengths and benefits of your brand. Then mark those that are most important to you and allow you to differ from your competitors. Now collect all key visual ideas that are possible matches for your brand (nature, history, animal kingdom and fairyland offer a vast fundus of possibilities). If necessary, ask incentive agencies for guidance. Qualities you should look for when choosing key visuals:

- Easily and quickly grasped
- Easy to understand
- Unique and distinctive
- Appeal to the emotions of the target group
- Different from the competition

'Create your own visual style ... let it be unique for yourself and yet identifiable for others.'

ORSON WELLES

Summary

☑ Key visuals offer a visual, unique position, fast assignment of the brand, and room for creative ideas.

☑ Key visuals are images you can use in campaigns to increase your recognition value.

☑ A specific key visual can become your trademark.

94

BUSINESS RITUALS WORLDWIDE

A GOOD BUSINESS CARD IS LIKE A KICK-ASS TIE

After meetings and presentations, people will often ask presenters for their business cards. There is no doubt that a business card is a necessity. With a business card you carry all important contact information about yourself with you, so don't overlook or undervalue your business card in marketing.

Business rituals look very different around the globe. In South Korea, for example, business cards are two-sided. One side is in Korean and the other side is in English. The Western-size business card has gradually become the standard around the world, although there are many countries that still use variations of a larger card.

A business card is a small and portable marketing tool, and the quality and information reflect the cardholder and their company. Your business card should reflect your company design, logo and brand identity. A good business card is like a kick-ass tie: it won't make you a better person, but it will get you some respect. By giving contacts your business card you are making it easy for them to retrieve information about you. Plus, the reverse side can be used to add more information or a marketing message.

A few tips for creating a good business card:

- Choose quality card stock with a good surface feel
- Make sure all abbreviations are consistent
- Keep titles consistent
- Be consistent with upper- and lowercase text
- Develop system formats.

'Good design is good business.'

THOMAS J WATSON

Summary

☑ Never underestimate what a business card can do for you.

☑ Invest time and money in creating a great design.

☑ Ensure that your business card conveys trustworthiness and makes an impact at the same time.

95

CREATE A GREAT LINKEDIN PROFILE

STAND OUT FROM THE CROWD

Linkedln is the perfect business platform, so you should create a great LinkedIn profile. LinkedIn, unlike most social media platforms, is not the place for posting cat content, or informing contacts about your latest meal. It is not the place for socialising with your friends or sharing your weekend experiences. LinkedIn is a business tool and should be treated as such.

As there are millions of users on this platform, it is necessary that you do everything to stand out from the crowd. The best way to do this is having a truly exceptional profile. A great LinkedIn profile will improve your visibility, and attract prospects and contacts.

Adam Houlahan, LinkedIn expert, bestselling author, international keynote speaker, and founder of the 12-Week Influencer Program can help you to succeed on LinkedIn. In his book, *The LinkedIn Playbook: Contacts to Customers. Engage. Connect. Convert*, he shares important tips for creating a successful LinkedIn profile, and I strongly recommend that you follow his advice. Adam's top tips:

- Your LinkedIn profile is *not* your resume: Don't think of LinkedIn as your curriculum vitae. When reading through your profile, it should not read as such.
- Write in the first person: Forget about writing in the third person in your summary and position descriptions. It's too impersonal. Always write in the first person.
- Keyword optimisation: Do some research and optimise your profile with regard to keywords. Search engines will concentrate on those specific keywords, which means people will be more likely to find you.
- Use your best job title: Think about a great job title in order to stand out. Do some research, look at what your competitors do. Avoid titles like CEO and general manager. A wrong title can be a big blow to your visibility.
- Invest time in secondary keywords: Don't overlook secondary keywords, which you should use to some degree in various areas of your profile. Don't see endorsements for specific skills on your profile as skills. Think of them as secondary keywords (you can have up to fifty skills).
- Use a professional headshot: Pictures really do speak a thousand words. Go to a photographer for a professional profile image. Ensure the background of the headshot is plain, with nothing behind you. Have the shot taken in a well-lit area. Let the photographer focus on your eyes, which should

be above the middle of the image. The correct file size of the headshot should be 500 x 500 pixels.

- Use a great profile background: Invest time in creating a great profile background that fits you and your work. The correct size of the background image is 1400 x 425 pixels.
- Come up with a professional headline: The headline should be well chosen as it sits in the area directly below your name. You have 120 characters to play with. You can use keywords separated by icons, or write a flowing sentence that includes your main keywords and expresses what your work is about.
- Select your country and the industry in which you work.
- Choose your special profile URL: Change the original URL that LinkedIn offers you to a unique and perfect URL.
- Make your profile public: You want to be seen so make your profile visible to everyone.
- Edit the contact information: Here you will see four options that are visible only to your first-level contacts: email address, phone number, IM and address. In an additional section you can add Twitter, WeChat and up to three websites.
- Summary: This section is important for a LinkedIn profile. It is your opportunity to get somebody interested in you. Here you have 2000 characters to play with. Your summary should concentrate on these points to tell people something about you:
  - Name
  - Claim to fame
  - Insight
  - Result you want to deliver
  - Experience
  - Problems you want to solve
  - How you will solve the problems

- ○ Your *why* (the reason why you are in business)
  - ○ Call to action
- Work experience: Add your current position, and any previous positions you have held. You have 2000 characters to use. Choose your title carefully. The title is about your keywords. Topics you could cover:
  - ○ Why your business exists
  - ○ How you solve problems
  - ○ What you do
  - ○ Call to action
- Languages: Which languages do you speak? How do you speak them (fluently, haltingly)?
- Skills and endorsements: Add skills that are relevant for you and your work. You can add up to fifty skills. People can give you endorsements here.
- Additional information: Add some keywords or share some interests.
- Education: Never leave this section blank or you will show up in fewer search results. List your important education points and awards. You can also add links to your school, university and training institutions.
- Recommendations: Ask your business partners and clients for recommendations. Make it easy for them and send them a link. Recommendations are a great way to boost your reputation.
- Join groups on LinkedIn: There are many interesting groups on LinkedIn. The best ones to join are those that contain your ideal clients. Or open up your own group where you can show your expertise.
- Follow influencers: There are many people worth following on LinkedIn. Influencers will not readily accept your contact

request, but by following their profile you can have access to their posts and status updates.

- All-star profile: There are five kind of profile rankings: beginner, intermediate, advanced, expert, and all-star (you should focus on completing your profile to receive an all-star profile).
- Add optional sections.

'One of the greatest challenges companies face in adjusting to the impact of social media, is knowing, where to start.'

SIMON MAINWARING

Summary

☑ A great LinkedIn profile will help with your visibility, and attract prospects and contacts.

☑ When your profile is optimised correctly it will speak to your ideal clients in the way they understand and are looking for.

☑ Put everything into creating a great LinkedIn profile.

THE LAW OF RESPECT

WHEN PEOPLE RESPECT YOU
THEY WILL FOLLOW YOU

Respected leaders know that they cannot just walk into a room and say, 'Hi, I am a leader. Follow me.' That will not work. The followers and people such a person attracts will not follow them by choice. They will love the person's advice and ideas, but they are still involuntary followers.

Leaders understand that to lead effectively and successfully they need to have the ability to attract people who want to follow them. Leaders recognise their need to attract followers. In order to understand leadership, we must understand and learn something about followership. People must feel confident in following. They must trust the leader. They must feel safe. The leader must clearly communicate the direction of their leadership, the outcomes desired, and the strategies to reach the outcomes. A good leader does what is right, and is even willing to stand alone occasionally. They do not fear failure and criticism.

A leader's courage gives followers hope, and a good leader always empowers their followers. Good leaders rely on respect, including showing respect for others, even when the other person has less power or is in a lower position. If a leader respects others and consistently leads them with respect, people will be more likely to respect and follow them.

It is also a fact that people respect those with success. They respect other's accomplishments and merits. Followers follow leaders who have success because they want to be a part of that success in the future. Good leadership means adding value to others. And followers value these leaders. They respect them.

When people respect you as a leader, they will follow you. 'Followers are attracted to people who are better leaders than themselves. That is the Law of Respect,' says John C Maxwell, bestselling author and speaker on leadership.

> *'When people respect you as a person, they admire you. When they respect you as a friend, they love you. When they respect you as a leader, they follow you.'*

JOHN C MAXWELL

Summary

☑ A Key Person of Trust is respected, attracts people and dream customers, and makes contacts easily through their leadership, personality and presentation.

☑ If people respect you as a leader they will follow you.

THE LAW OF ATTRACTION

ATTRACT MORE OF WHAT YOU FOCUS ON

The Law of Attraction uses the power of the mind to translate whatever is in your thoughts and turn them into reality. That means that all your thoughts turn into things eventually. If you focus on negative things, you will remain under that negative cloud. If you focus on positive thoughts and have goals, you will find a way to achieve those goals through action. This principle can be summarised as follows:

- If you focus on how bad life is, life becomes worse.
- If you focus on how good life is, live improves.
- If you focus on opportunities, you get more opportunities.

The Law of Attraction teaches that like attracts like. You've heard of Buddha. Buddha was so impressive that an entire religion sprang forth from his philosophy. Buddha not only knew about the Law of Attraction, but taught it as well.

Here are a few of Buddha's lessons:

- We create our own reality. What we are today comes from our thoughts of yesterday, and our present thoughts build our life of tomorrow. Our life is the creation of our mind.
- We create our own health. Every human being is the author of his own health and disease.
- We create our own enemies. An outside enemy exists only if there is anger inside.
- We create our own happiness. We are shaped by our thoughts; we become what we think. When the mind is pure, joy follows like a shadow that never leaves.
- We create our own abilities. He is able who thinks he is able.

'As a man thinketh in his heart so is he.'

PROVERBS 23:7

Summary

☑ We can all create our own reality, happiness and success.

☑ Our thoughts can influence our success.

☑ Learn to use the Law of Attraction to achieve success.

98

DO YOU ATTRACT FOLLOWERS OR LEADERS?

A DIFFERENT FOCUS

There are two kinds of leaders, those who attract followers and those who attract other leaders. This difference is important, because people who only attract followers will never be able to influence people. They will only have shallow contact. But leaders who attract other leaders can deeply influence others and are able to multiply their successes. For attracting other leaders you need a different mindset. Concentrate on attracting leaders; they are the real chance for success.

Traits of leaders who attract followers only:

- Want to be needed
- Need recognition
- Treat everyone the same
- Focus on people's weaknesses
- Spend time with others
- Develop the bottom 20 percent
- Have some success

Traits of leaders who attract other leaders:

- Want others to have success
- Want to reproduce themselves
- Treat individuals differently
- Focus on other people's strengths
- Invest time in others
- Develop the top 20 percent
- Have incredible success

'Just because you attract followers doesn't mean you have influence.'

KARIN SEBELIN

Summary

☑ Being able to attract other leaders will give you a real chance of success.

99

HOW TO ATTRACT INFLUENCERS

FOCUS ON INFLUENCER MARKETING

An integrated approach to influencer marketing delivers great return on investment (ROI). People do care what influencers do, what they eat and wear and who they date. The power influencers have can be leveraged for your own branding efforts.

Influencers are not only hugely talented, but they have often built large audiences and fan bases by sharing their talent with the world. They create the best content, know how to engage with large audiences, and interact in a way that incites action. Influencers, by having our trust, can influence our decision-making. They can get us to think about something differently.

Generally, influencers will have a large, loyal following, are authorities (top experts in their field), are trusted, and have success through their impressive results. Here are some myths about influencers:

- It takes years to become an influencer
- Have to be famous
- Have to be attractive
- Have to be talented
- Need great technical skills
- Need to be discovered
- Have succeeded due to luck, which cannot be planned

Becoming an influencer is not about becoming the next Richard Branson. You can rise to an influencer level and make a fulfilling living without becoming the next famous billionaire. Not all influencers are equal. There are different types of influencers and they value different things. When you understand what each influencer values, you will have more success in reaching out to influencers.

There are several important types of influencers:

- Bloggers/vloggers: Are active on a variety of social media channels, and can provide springboards for others' campaigns. Bloggers write on niche-based topics allowing marketers to find influencers, who have a very targeted audience. Blogs comprise the top five sources of trustworthy information. The average buyer consults eleven product reviews before making a purchase decision; most of these reviews are blog posts.
- Celebrities: Actors, filmmakers, musicians, sportspeople or gaming enthusiasts who have skills companies can leverage.

All they have to do to inspire people to buy the product is hold it near their face and take a nice photo.

- Influential thought leaders/authorities: Have expertise, practise thought leadership, enjoy massive influence and can move something.
- PR influencers: Editors, journalists, PR people.
- Connectors: Have great networks and can make introductions to many people. They connect easily with other people.
- Micro-influencers: Popular social media stars who have made a name for themselves in a particular industry.

Your chance for success is influencer marketing. What is influencer marketing? It is a kind of marketing that focuses on using key leaders or influencers to drive a brand's message to a larger marketing. Instead of marketing directly to consumers, you inspire, hire or pay influencers to get the word out for you. The result can be influencer campaigns, whereby influencers are expected to spread the word through their social media channels. Influencers can be influential in the following ways:

- Bloggers/vloggers
- Thought leaders
- Entrepreneurs
- Authors
- Editors/journalists
- Analysts
- Podcasters
- Coaches/trainers
- Musicians
- Sportspeople/athletes

- Actors
- Models
- TV stars
- Celebrities
- Photographers

Influencers can be reached in various ways:

- Bloggers/vloggers: Reaching out to potential bloggers is a more intricate process now than in former years. Great bloggers are constantly getting pitched to by marketers so it is important that you stand out from the crowd if you want them to pay attention. First, do some research. Identify the right bloggers and the types of content each blogger is currently creating to earn a living. They could mention your product on their blog, or host a blogger-friendly PR event or Twitter chat. Second, reach out to bloggers in a personalised manner. Ask the bloggers/vloggers you want to work with for ideas on how you can partner. Send a personalised pitch that contains the following:
  - Brief background on you, your business and your brand
  - Reasons why you are a good fit
  - What you are asking of the blogger, specifically what you would like them to do for your brand
  - What you are willing to give in a mutually beneficial relationship
  - Link to brand assets (awesome content, brand items, infographics, exclusive interviews) (in further emails)
  - Help promoting the campaign, which you can share on your own channels for better exposure.

308

Use common sense and be straightforward. Your messaging needs to be as succinct as possible. Be passionate about what you are pitching. Be creative.

- Celebrities: Celebrities are the hardest influencers to connect with. Reaching out to a celebrity is often a long-term game and the process can be very time consuming. It can take great effort on your part to get an answer to emails. Celebrities rarely answer their own emails or phone calls. They often have gatekeepers, such as receptionists or managers whose primary focus is to safeguard the valuable time of the celebrity for more relevant opportunities. If you want to be successful in reaching out to a celebrity, first appear respectful to the gatekeeper. Remember that the gatekeeper is a person, too, and also has goals, aspirations, dreams and a life to lead. Show genuine interest in them. Try to find out what role they play in connecting people with the celebrity. When you have established rapport with the gatekeeper, then you can ask to get in front of the influencer. But beware: the more well known a celebrity is, the more expensive they will be to work with.

- Authority influencers: These influencers often write articles, host podcasts, do video series, do speaking gigs, write books or give seminars. Your goal here is to help them increase their authority by supporting them and engaging with them. Podcasts, for example, are a good way to reach out to such authority influencers.

- PR influencers: We all want to get into the media. For start-ups, especially, getting press from PR influencers can be a golden ticket. Although media coverage isn't the major growth driver, the press can be good for kickstarting your business and increasing your brand value. Connecting with journalists is not so easy because they get many email pitches every day. The good news is that most pitches are poor. Here some important points for reaching out to PR influencers:

- Know the people who write about your industry and start building real relationships with them.
- Put them on a first-to-know list for when you have a new product or announcement.
- Don't use flattery to achieve your goal. Instead, use knowledge about their publication.
- Pay careful attention to the kinds of stories the publication runs.
- Pitching to a journalist is not about blatant self-promotion. Journalists aren't concerned with what's good for you but what is good for their readers. They are interested in driving traffic to their articles. They are also interested in exclusive stories, which lead to more traffic.
- Learn to think like an editor or journalist.
- Get your pitch right with the first email.

   Because PR people are bombarded with pitches they don't have the incentive to dive deeply into any individual one. This means you only have a few sentences to hook them, and you have to do it in the first email by explaining what makes you and your story interesting and relevant to their readers. Whether or not you are successful with a PR influencer depends on whether they are publication writer or freelancer, the prestige of the publication/s they write for, and the size of their audience.

- Connectors: The biggest value connectors bring is their relationships with other influencers in their networks. Connectors value deep relationships and connections. But this does not mean they will do everything for you. As with any influencer you reach out to, you need to communicate the value to connectors. It can be hard to measure the impact connectors have so it's not always ideal to target them for a campaign.

- Micro-influencers: These people are often described as 'the long tail of the power law' (the 'head' consists of celebrities). The rising trend in influencer marketing is to work with such micro-influencers. When reaching out to micro-influencers, think of quality rather than quantity. A micro-influencer who doesn't have thousands of followers could be a better influencer resource than a major celebrity you can't afford anyway.

  Micro-influencers are more likely to respond to your pitch because they receive fewer requests. If you are new to influencer marketing, this may be a good chance for you. If you treat micro-influencers with respect, they will be more likely to connect with you. Rolling out the red carpet for a micro-influencer is your chance that this influencer will go the extra mile for you. Since micro-influencers often have a higher engagement as other influencers, this often leads to higher sales. HelloSociety, for example, found out that micro-influencers had a 60 percent higher engagement rate compared to regular influencers.

It's good to know that in general all influencers are interested in a pay-to-play model. Bloggers, on the other hand, tend to be less interested in receiving money. That could have something to do with Google's policy on buying links. However, that does not mean they don't want to be paid. You should be careful, how you approach the subject.

Social media influencers often generate better ROI for B2C business, and blogging influencers are often better for B2B business. Some useful tools for blogger and influencer outreach:

- BirdSong Analytics
- BuzzSumo
- TwtrLand
- Circloscope
- Tomoson
- MyBlogU
- TwChat

> *'To work with influencers requires engagement and creativity from you.'*

EVY WILKINS

Summary

☑ Reaching influencers and your audience through influencers should be on your to-do list.

☑ Influencer marketing can give you the chance for success.

☑ Learn to differentiate the kind of influencers, and how to reach out to them.

THE FIVE
RELATIONSHIP
CIRCLES

NEVER STOP IMPROVING
YOUR RELATIONSHIPS

Leaders do not succeed alone, and often their potential is determined by the people closest to them. What makes the difference is the leader's inner circle. Not everyone recognises that those people closest to them will make or break them. There are still leaders who believe in the concept of the Lone Ranger as their model for leadership. There are no Lone Ranger leaders. Why? When you lead alone, you don't lead anybody.

Most people create an inner circle of people. We normally surround ourselves with people we like or people we feel comfortable. We often don't show consideration for the fact that our direct environment shapes us and, in the end, our success.

Do you know that you are the sum of the five people closest you? They shape you, to a greater or lesser degree. Who are you drawing into your inner circle? Who is in your direct circles? Are you sure the right people are around you?

To practise effective relationship building, you must be intentional in your relationship building. If you want to reach your full potential as a leader you should know who is in your circles, should know, why certain people are in your circles, and what you can do to influence them. Your inner circle should comprise those people you seek out for advice, turn to for support and rely on to help you.

Mari Smith has described in her book, *The New Relationship Marketing*, the concept of 'The Five Relationship Circles'. The idea is that you map out all your current and potential contacts in concentric circles, beginning with those you are closest to and then moving to the periphery of people you do not yet know.

The Five Relationship Circles:

1. Intimates: These are your very close friends, people with whom you share a great deal of mutual love and respect. With them you share your secrets and your problems. You trust them to look after your home and your children. You can call them at midnight. They are there for you and support you.
2. Friends: These are the people with whom you interact regularly. You have shared interests. You trust and respect these people. If you were planning a party, you would invite them.
3. Key contacts: In this circle are your professional contacts. You know these people fairly well, but not much about their

private lives. People in this circle are experts, and are considered influencers. Some of them might even be your clients.

4. Acquaintances: This is the largest group of people. These are people you know peripherally. In this circle could be most of your friends, fans and followers from social media. You could know some of them from your email list, or have done business with them.

5. Community at large: The last circle includes people you don't yet know. This is your target market, and includes prospective clients.

When you map out your current and potential contacts in circles you can identify those you want to upgrade or even downgrade. You might want to host a free webinar to allow your community at large to get to know you better. Or you could identify some Twitter followers who are coming up in their field of expertise and reach out to help them. You could also deepen your relationships by key contacts by sending meaningful gifts pertaining to their interests. Another idea would be writing thank-you cards to special people for being remembered.

'Treasure your relationships, not your possessions.'

ANTHONY J D'ANGELO

Summary

☑ A good leader is intentional in their relationship building.

☑ Work on your circles to make effective connections and nurture relationships. Also give people the chance to come into your circles.

☑ Great inner circles do not come together by accident.

☑ Good leaders are continually developing current and future inner-circle members.

☑ Examine your list of inner-circle members and determine who should be there.

☑ The Five Relationship Circles concept will help you build social equity and reward you.

THE IMPORTANCE OF THOUGHT LEADERSHIP

IT'S NOT ENOUGH TO BE AN EXPERT

Many people think that being an expert will make them successful, but that thinking is false. Gone are the times when it was sufficient for someone to call themselves an expert and exert their dominance through the pressure of advertising. We now need thought leaders. Whoever wants to position themselves as a thought leader today needs a vision, and a mission that offers clear value for the customer.

First we should clarify the term *thought leader*. A thought leader is someone who is known and respected for having extraordinary expertise in their field. Thought leadership can be personally identifiable or organisation based. This means that a person can take the role of a thought leader or an organisation as a whole.

A good definition of the terms 'expert' and 'thought leader' is in the book, *The Thought Leaders Practice*, by Matt Church, Peter Cook and Scott Stein. The book defines thought leadership as 'thinking in action'. It claims that 'we have moved our need from information knowledge to applied wisdom; from expert to trusted authority'. In the book, there are two definitions:

- An expert: someone who knows something
- A thought leader: someone who is known for knowing something

See the difference? From this, we can say that thought leaders are meaning makers, and are able to influence others.

Nowadays it is not enough to have a PhD, which simply means having very deep knowledge in a narrow field, being an expert in that field. Information is now available to us all. It's the ability to draw meaning and application from that information that builds higher value. We must start to take what we know and make it more valuable to others. We must go from knowing stuff to being known for knowing stuff. We must go from having answers to being able to create the need.

According to the Institute for the Future, 'sensemaking' is one of the ten key skills necessary for the future of work (Future Work Skills 2020). The word 'sensemaking' means the ability to determine the deeper meaning or significance of what is being expressed. Sensemaking belongs to the skills of a thought leader, not an expert. When we are able to align our own expertise to the problems and challenges we are experiencing, when we can persuade through sensemaking, we are a thought leader.

Knowledge is no competitive advantage anymore. But knowing how to apply that knowledge to achieve a specific outcome is a definite advantage. But don't assume that being a thought leader means knowing everything. A thought leader should be able to create new insights and repurpose old insights so that they are relevant. We must all learn to sell our ideas and expertise, or our intellectual property (IP), in a way that others value. In the end, a thought leader should be a trusted advisor.

There are many advantages to thought leadership:

- Attention
- Engagement: a thought leader attracts followers
- Attractiveness for employees, employers and cooperation partners
- Brand affinity: people are able to get to know us as a brand on neutral ground

'Thought leadership is when a leader's thoughts are being used by leaders to lead others.'

ONYI ANYADO

Summary

☑ It is not enough to be an expert nowadays.

☑ We need more thought leaders in the world. Or, as Einstein said so well: 'The problems that exist in the world today cannot be solved by the level of thinking that created them.'

BECOME A THOUGHT LEADER

THOUGHT LEADERS MUST PROVE THEMSELVES

A person cannot just stand up and declare, 'Hey, look at me, I'm a thought leader.' That will not work. 'Thought leaders do not become thought leaders by trying to be one; that's an external focus that only satisfies the ego and blocks true enlightenment on any subject. A thought leader has a singular, internal focus on achieving mastery of a particular discipline,' says Sam Fiorella.

We all would like to become thought leaders. But a thought leader gains their reputation by proving their own worth to others who know a lot about a particular industry. Thought leaders obtain credentials through education, knowledge and experience, and use this to help others. They are generally, as already mentioned, considered experts in their field of industry. Thought leaders must be able to provide new insight into different aspects of their expertise. A thought leader's views on a subject are taken to be authoritative and influential, and it's not easy to get into that position.

If you want to stand out and be a true thought leader, you should offer your audience something different, including new information and disruptive ideas that would stir things up. Guy Kawasaki, former evangelist of Apple, says, 'A thought leader is someone who creates something before people realise that they need it. Best example, of course, is Steve Jobs. Richard Branson, too.'

Thought leaders are able to aggregate followers around ideas to educate, influence and inspire. Now you probably want to know if anyone can become a thought leader. Yes, through hard work, dedication and creativity, almost anyone can become a thought leader. It means having a powerful and visible brand and then taking those aspects of their personal brand to a higher level.

Matt Sweetwood, CEO, C-Suite advisor, life coach and Lumix photographer, who has gained a reputation as a thought leader, shares a few tips on how to become a thought leader:

- Love your topic and believe in it
- Be authentic
- Get experience
- Write, write, write
- Ask for help
- Be social
- Use live video
- Network in person
- Be bold and pitch yourself to media
- Put in time and effort

A thought leader concentrates on their topic, and collects and curates as much information as possible. They are focused on their target group, which is very important, and considers their needs whenever possible. A thought leader regularly shares interesting content in the networks via their website, features in magazines and newspapers, and also speaks at conferences and events.

Important skills for thought leadership are passion, vision, mission, expertise, experience, ambitiousness, persistence, curiosity, and self-confidence. Successful thought leaders spend much time with research reading articles and books, listening to podcasts, and watching videos. They are always on the lookout for new inspiration.

Follow these tips and you will be on a good way to becoming a thought leader.

> *'Thought leaders are the informed opinion leaders and the go-to people in their field of expertise. They are trusted sources who move and inspire people with innovative ideas.'*

DENISE BROSSEAU

Summary

☑ If you want to become a thought leader you must first prove yourself. To do this, you need to develop a powerful and visible brand.

THE SECRETS OF TEAM SUCCESS

THE VALUE OF EFFECTIVE TEAMS

Building strong, effective teams is critical to business success. It takes great leadership to build effective teams. However, effective team management can lead to great success for the team and the organisation. It can lead to better outcomes, increased efficiency, improved ideas, mutual support, higher motivation, increased competency, and a sense of accomplishment. Some tips for effective team management and great team success:

- Lead by example
- Appreciate each team member
- Set standards
- Communicate effectively

- Avoid criticism
- Give effective and honest feedback
- Avoid favouritism
- Motivate team members
- Give credit when necessary
- Reward where it's due
- Allow your team members to take risks
- Let people make mistakes
- Involve people in processes
- Do not make decisions alone
- Align group goals with organisational goals
- Manage conflicts
- Have periodic assessments
- Maintain discipline

'Great things in business are never done by one person. They're done by a team of people.'

STEVE JOBS

Summary

☑ We rely on ourselves too much, and often want to do everything alone.

☑ To be seen as a trustworthy leader and role model, we should include others in the process; we should build teams.

☑ Building effective teams can lead to great success for the team and the organisation.

KEY QUALITY 7: DEVELOP A PERSONAL VOICE, MESSAGE, MISSION AND VISION

BUILD, MAINTAIN AND DRIVE BRAND AWARENESS

In today's world success involves building a brand that connects emotionally with others in a way that aligns with its goals. Be passionate about finding your creative voice and building this presence. Find your personal voice, message, mission and vision in order to build, maintain and drive brand awareness.

A few key points about brand awareness:

- Brand voice: Today everyone has a voice. We should learn to better utilise our voice. And brand voice doesn't mean audio logos, sound effects or theme songs. It means the tone of your communication and the style of your writing. A brand voice offers the chance of engaging and motivating your audience through purposeful and consistent expression using words and prose style. Your personality is, to a larger extent, determined by the words you use and the sentences you write. Learn to create an authentic voice for your brand.

- Brand message: Your brand message is the core of your brand. It is the basis of all your efforts and strategies, resulting in a cohesive, consistent and clear brand. Through your brand message you can relay your underlying brand value and brand proposition through the right language, content and efforts that will inspire, appeal to and persuade your target market.

- Mission: Also called mission statement, this defines and guides the future state that you are striving for as a brand. A mission statement is a mindset that continually drives your business forward. Start-ups often confuse their mission with their brand's positioning strategy, but they are meant to serve two completely different purposes. Your mission statement is built for your organisation. It should serve as a north star to guide and motivate your employees, and your team, making sure they stay focused.

- Vision: A brand vision helps guide the future. It supports a business strategy, differentiates the business from competitors, resonates with customers, and inspires employees and partners. It can be the basis for developing marketing programs.

'Stay strong. Have a voice,
message, mission, vision.'

KARIN SEBELIN

Summary

☑ The 7th Key Quality of a Key Person of Trust is developing a great personal voice, message, mission and vision for your brand.

☑ Invest time and money in your brand voice, message, mission and vision.

FIND YOUR BRAND VOICE AND MESSAGE

FIND A WAY TO CONNECT WITH CONSUMERS

Now we'll talk about brand voice and brand message. Your brand voice is your special connection to the world. It is dependent on your company's mission, audience and industry. Success is all about how you communicate with people—prospects and customers—and how they respond to you.

A brand voice could be:

- Professional
- Authoritative
- Friendly
- Conversational

- Informative
- Promotional
- Technical
- Service-oriented

There are many possibilities for building a brand voice behind your message. In the end, you need to choose a brand voice that makes sense and resonates with your target group, in other words a brand voice that achieves its aims. Keep in mind that it's important to connect with consumers. This is extremely important when writing and publishing blog articles, and sharing social media posts.

A consistent brand voice will help your brand image to success. It will help you become recognised as an expert and thought leader. Use the business voice that fits with your mission and vision.

Let's explain the term 'brand message' now. The brand message—philosophy, slogan—is behind every great brand, and is a philosophy that sets it apart. Your brand message should be intricately associated to your business and brand. It should be centred on the vision and values of your company. Building a brand message is an opportunity for communication on a personal and human level. It can create an emotional connection with your consumers.

A brand message communicates your company's *why*. A brand message tells people who you are, what you have to offer, why people should pick your product or service, and why you do your work. Your brand message should be distinctive, short, simple and clear. If someone speaks about your philosophy without mentioning your brand name, others should quickly realise that the person was speaking about you.

When creating a brand message, be careful not to address what your products and services can do. Instead, address why they are important to your customers. Our brand message sounds like this: 'Becoming a Key Person of Trust (KPT) - The Next Revolution in Branding.' It's short, simple and clear. Everyone knows why we are so special.

What is the message that you convey to the world?

'Your brand voice is an expression of the people behind your brand.'

KARIN SEBELIN

'A brand is a person that has a voice, evokes emotion and spreads a message.'

RICHIE NORTO

Summary

☑ Develop a consistent brand voice and message to build trust.

☑ Your voice is dependent on your company's mission, audience and industry.

☑ Your brand message should be distinctive, short, simple and clear and should communicate your company's *why*.

DEVELOP YOUR ELEVATOR PITCH

HOW TO PERSUADE IN SIXTY SECONDS

An elevator pitch is a short presentation that helps persuade prospects or investors. The elevator pitch was originally the idea of American salesmen with the aim of making a sale to customers and bosses during an elevator ride. Most elevator rides lasted for about sixty seconds, so all relevant information had to fit into this time span.

If someone asks you what you do for a living, what do you answer? Do you give a long explanation? Do you tell your whole business story? Or do you concentrate on a few sentences that explain briefly what your profession is? It's a fact that people don't like it when someone speaks in long sentences and does not stop talking.

We all have our individual pain barriers. Our attention spans are often limited. Therefore you should learn to introduce yourself in a few short sentences. When giving a presentation, show your enthusiasm for the project. Seize your chance and present yourself via a great elevator pitch. You can use an elevator pitch for meetings (networking), job interviews, casual contacts, phone calls and fairs.

You can write a successful elevator pitch by following the AIDA concept (attention, interest, desire, action):

- Attention: Create attention by saying what you have to offer your counterpart. What is new?
- Interest: Create interest by explaining your unique selling proposition (USP). How do you differ from others? What is your niche?
- Desire: Create desire by explaining the benefits you offer. What advantages do your products and services have?
- Action: Provoke action by motivating your counterpart. Tell them what they should do.

A great elevator pitch does not fall from heaven. You should be prepared ahead of time for when you need it. The first sentence is crucial. The whole pitch should be brief, no longer than thirty to sixty seconds, and should contain your name and your company. A few helpful tips to making a successful elevator pitch:

- Create a great opening
- Prioritise content
- Be persuasive
- Share your skills
- Point out specialities and advantages
- Explain what makes you special
- Talk clearly and distinctly

- Show excitement and joy
- Be authentic
- Don't speak too fast
- Don't talk in monologues
- Mention your goals
- End with a call to action
- Have a business card ready

Here a good example of an elevator pitch: 'My name is Sarah Parker, and I create illustrations for websites and brands. My passion is finding creative ways to express a message, and drawing illustrations that people share on social media.'

Summary

☑ An elevator pitch is a great way to share your expertise and credentials quickly and effectively with people who don't know you.

☑ Develop an interesting elevator pitch.

☑ Follow the AIDA concept.

☑ An elevator pitch should be brief, and should contain your name and your company's name.

☑ Exercise the presentation of your elevator pitch.

☑ Practise, practise, practise.

DEFINE YOUR VISION AND MISSION

WRITE A VISION AND A MISSION STATEMENT

Your mission and vision should be part of the core of your business plan. When people read through your vision and mission statement, they will know what your business does and how you help people, where you are going and how you plan to get there. In order to write your vision and mission statements, you need to know what is inside your strategic plan.

Follow the following two steps to create your vision and mission statements (always begin with your vision):

1. Your vision statement: This explains where your business is headed, where it will be in the future. It also provides guidance for the

day-to-day process of running your business. A vision statement is rooted in the future, and provides direction and inspiration. Your vision relates to seeing and looking, thus vision statements are about looking ahead. Your vision defines in a few sentences or phrases your business goals. A vision statement should be written in plain, everyday language. Avoid business jargon. A vision statement is aspirational, inspirational and motivational.

What is your long-term goal? What will your business look like in the future? In five years, in ten years? Dove, the company that sells beauty products, has the following vision: 'We believe beauty should be a source of confidence, and not anxiety. That's why we are here to help women everywhere develop a positive relationship with the way they look, helping them raise their self-esteem and realise their full potential.'

Follow these steps to write your own vision statement:

- Revisit your strategic plan. Think about your elevator pitch, business values, business goals, business strengths and opportunities, and your business story.
- Create a vision board, and ask yourself:
  - Who does my business help?
  - What is the purpose of my business?
  - How do I want to make the world a better place with my business?
  - What problems does my business solve?
  - What is my ultimate aim for my business?
- Make a summary and create something special from it.
- Use short words and sentences, and concrete language.
- Continually review your vision statement for improvement.

2. Your mission statement: Your mission statement can provide you with guidance. Your mission statement explains what your business needs to do in day-to-day operations to make your

vision statement a reality. Your mission statement is rooted in the present and is practical. It defines in a few sentences or a phrase the practical things you will do to achieve your vision statement. It is about what you do and who/what you do this for. With its practical focus, such a mission statement is easier to write than a vision statement. Ask yourself:

- Why does my business exist?
- What is the purpose of my business?
- Is there an egoistic *why* or a societal *why*?
- What inspires me the most in life?
- What annoys me the most in life?
- What are my principles in life?

Each mission statement implies that somebody is helped. Be clear about whom you want to help, whom you want to inspire (economy, politics, science, research, journalism).

Here is Dove's mission statement: 'The Dove Self-Esteem Project was created from a vision where beauty is a source of confidence, not anxiety. We've reached over 20 million young people with self-esteem education, and together we can reach 20 million more. Our mission is to ensure that the next generation grows up enjoying a positive relationship with the way they look – helping young people raise their self-esteem and realise their full potential. We've partnered with leading experts in the fields of psychology, health and body image to create a program of evidence based resources including parenting advice to help young people form healthy friendships, overcome body image issues and be their best selves.'

Follow these steps to write your mission statement:

- Focus on the customer; ask yourself what you should do for your customers to make your vision a reality

- Use short words and sentences and concrete language (fifteen to twenty words will work best)
- Your mission statement should be clear and easy to understand
- Your mission statement should be easy to remember
- Your mission statement needs verbs as activity
- Continually review your mission statement for improvement

Summary

☑ Write your vision and mission statements to put your business on the right track for success.

☑ A vision statement is rooted in the future, and provides direction and inspiration.

☑ Your mission statement explains what your business must do in day-to-day operations to make your vision statement a reality.

SHARE YOUR BRAND STORY

IDENTIFY YOUR PERSONAL BRAND STORY

The best brands are built on great stories. What is a brand story? A brand story is more than content; it is a narrative. It's more than the content on a website, the text in a brochure, and more than a presentation to investors.

Your personal brand story is what people believe about you based on the signals sent by you and your brand. A brand story is the whole picture made up of facts, experiences, emotions and interpretations. It is not only the story you tell. There are also the colours and texture of your business cards, and many other elements add to the package of your brand story. Every element should reflect your personality and your story. What kind of story will you tell?

Reasons why you need to tell your brand story:

- Having no special story to tell means you are a replaceable business on the market. You have no way to differentiate yourself from others. But with a brand story you are able to stand out and get noticed.
- People will learn to care about you and your business and want to buy into it.
- Your brand story is all about framing the value you bring to the market.
- Your brand story is about striving for the creation of loyalty, and the creation of meaningful bonds with your customers. A great brand story increases brand awareness.
- Your brand story is no catchy content that is written on a wall for two weeks. It is the foundation of your brand and the strategy for your future growth.

To read my brand story, go to keypersonoftrust.de/my-success-story. How can you wrap your message in a story? How did you get to where you are now?

'In life it's not what happens to you. It's what you become because of it.'

KARIN SEBELIN

Summary

- [✓] It doesn't matter what kind of business you have, you have a unique brand story to tell. It's your job to give your customers a story to tell.

- [✓] Create a compelling brand story.

- [✓] Develop a great concept that unites your brand name, product names, book titles and more in your brand story.

CREATE COMPELLING BRAND EXPERIENCES

BRAND EXPERIENCE IS THE FUTURE OF MARKETING

Not so long ago, the approach many brands took was to sell and forget. Brands sold their products and services, the customers went away, and the contact was complete until the next transaction. That has changed. Now most brands aim on a continuous engagement with their audience.

Brands have realised how important brand loyalty is to the growth of their business, and that compelling brand experiences are the way to success.

What is brand experience? Marty Neumeier, author of *The Dictionary of Brand*, defined it as 'all the interaction people have with a product, service, or organisation; the raw material of a brand'.

Why brand experiences? People have become relatively immune to targeted messages. The appropriate way to reach them is to create an experience within them. A memorable experience generates buzz and is fun to share. Compelling brand experiences attract customers and extend customer loyalty. Experiences you create should be distinct economic offerings that engage your customers and create memories within them. The brand experience should create connections to the real world by sensing the context of the customer. Some suggestions for creating a positive brand experience:

- Repeat the message of your brand consistently and frequently.
- Select the most effective touch points to deliver your message (a touch point is a person, place, thing or situation that facilitates contact between your brand and your ideal clients and is the point where your brand comes into contact with the right people. Examples of touch points: websites and blogs, presentations, blast emails, direct mail, advertising campaigns, apps).
- Create a meaningful, relevant and distinctive touchpoint execution: Make the most of your product concepts, appearance and user interaction to grab your audience's attention and fully communicate your brand message.

For a brand, the ultimate question is: 'How likely is it that a consumer would recommend our company and products to a friend or colleague?' Positive brand experiences are the key to success. When a person recommends your product to their friend, you can be happy. Good recommendations are everything.

'It is the experience a brand creates and curates, through its products and services that defines it in the mind of customers.'

NATHAN WILLIAM, SENIOR STRATEGIST WOLFF OLINS

Summary

☑ Create compelling brand experiences.

☑ View every interaction with prospective customers as an opportunity.

☑ Brand experience is the future of marketing.

DEVELOP A CONTENT STRATEGY

DEFINING A CONTENT STRATEGY

You need content strategy because it guides the creation, delivery and governance of useful, usable content. It lays down the rules for creating and using content that you intend to follow, and establishes the tools and resources you will work with. Content marketing can help your business prepare and plan for reliable and cost-effective sources of website traffic and new leads. If you are able to create a steady amount of organic traffic with just one blog post, you are well on the way to success. Kevin P Nichols says: 'We define content strategy as: getting the right content to the right user at the right time.'

Your content strategy is the central piece of your marketing plan. There are three stages of content strategy:

1. Content planning: user personas, measurable goals
2. Content delivery: content calendar, content mapping, content creation
3. Content analytics: Google analytics, user experience, SEO
   When you develop a content strategy, consider the following:

- Who you are creating your content for
- The problem you want to solve for your audience
- How your solution will be unique
- The formats on which you will focus
- The channels where your content will be published
- How you will schedule and manage creation and publication

You also need to know what your important topics and keywords are, actualise existing articles, and integrate in your best content a call to action for a lead magnet (an offer that you can promote to prospective customers in exchange for their email address or other forms of information).

'Content strategy encompasses the discovery, ideation, implementation and maintenance of all types of digital content: links, tags, metadata, video, whatever.'

ROBERT STRIBLEY, INFORMATION ARCHITECT AT RAZORFISH

Summary

☑ A well thought out content strategy is essential to doing business in today's market.

☑ The trend toward content marketing is increasing every day.

BEGIN BLOGGING

WHY YOU SHOULD BLOG

Now that you know about content strategy you can set up your own blog. What is a blog? According to Wikipedia, a blog (a truncation of the expression 'weblog') is a discussion or informational website published on the World Wide Web consisting of discrete, often informal diary-style text entries or posts. Posts are typically displayed in reverse chronological order so the most recent post appears at the top of the web page. Ultimately, a blog is a content-management system with special functions. A blog should be the communication platform for your business.

Reasons to begin blogging:

- One of the most popular ways of communicating and spreading information and news
- Gives you the chance to express yourself and share information with others

- Can make you a better person and a better writer
- Google loves blogs (it is an opportunity being listed in search engines)
- Will bring you leads via email lists
- Opportunity to make money through blogging
- Enables you to position yourself as an expert

If you want to have success with your blog, here are some points to keep in mind:

- Ensure that your posts are not boring
- Create quality content
- Keep your content up to date
- Post content that leads to interaction
- Consider keywords when you post content
- Provide links to other valuable sites
- Concentrate on your niche
- Build on what works
- Make people stay or return to your blog
- Offer people (additional) value
- Extend your reach through industry forums or social media, and send out newsletters, release videos, or start podcasts

How to start your own blog:

- Choose a great blog platform (WordPress, Drupal, Blogger)
- Choose the right web host for your blog (self-hosted is better)
- Set up a blog on your own domain
- Design your new blog
- Use resources for blogging
- Customise your blog

I consider WordPress to be the best option. It's certainly the most used. The advantages of WordPress:

- Easy to set up
- Free to use
- Plenty of free themes and layouts
- Many plugins to install
- Great functionality
- Great support forum
- Content can be shared and commented on

A self-hosted blog is the best choice. A free blog via WordPress. com, Tumblr or Blogger won't cost you anything, but you don't own your own domain name, and you don't own your blog (what does that sound or look like: 'yourblog-wordpress.com'). And you can't fully monetise your blog. You can't upload all the videos and images you want because the possibilities are limited. And you don't have access to the free themes offered by WordPress.

You might ask which is the right web host for you. That is your own decision. There are many web-hosting companies on the market. Popular hosts are BlueHost, HostGator, and iPage. Since I am in Germany, I use Strato as my provider.

To set up a blog on your own domain, you'll need to come up with a domain name you like. The domain is basically the URL of your website. (For example: google.com is a domain name). Your web provider should have a button for a quick installation of the desired blog system. That button will install, for example, WordPress on your blog. And when your blog system is installed, all you have to do is log onto the blog system (for WordPress this login would look like this: www.yourblognamehere.com/wp-login.php).

After your blog is installed, you need a good theme design. In WordPress you can find free theme designs via the standard installation or the search function. You can also upload special themes. You should be able to find many theme-design companies offering good templates for an attractive price.

When your design is installed and customised, install some additional plugins that will bring you the desired results. Be careful not to install too many plugins because that could cause system problems. Always check whether your chosen plugin has been tested for your system. Finally, customise your blog (choose the right settings and add categories, a navigation menu, widgets, pages, etc.).

We've covered the most important points for setting up a blog. Now you are able to post your first blog article.

'I blog because I have something to say.'

EDDIE HUANG

Summary

☑ Work out what good content strategy looks like and begin blogging.

☑ A blog is the communication platform for your business.

☑ Choose a great blog platform and the right web host, then set up the blog, design it, and use resources to customise it.

112

DEVELOP A STRATEGY FOR SOCIAL MEDIA

WHY YOU NEED A SOCIAL MEDIA STRATEGY

Marketers often make the mistake of diving into social media without a clear plan. This attitude is certainly a mistake and can lead to a disaster. When it comes to social media, to be successful you need an effective, clearly defined strategy.

What does an effective social media (marketing) strategy look like? It is the summary of everything you plan to do and hope to achieve on social media. It guides your actions and lets you know whether you are successful or not. Every post, article, reply, like, and comment should serve a purpose. The more specific your strategy is, the more effective you will be. Here a few tips to help you get started:

- Understand your goals: What is the purpose of your efforts? Who do you want to reach? What are your objectives?
- Create measurable objectives: Focus on the SMART strategy when setting goals. Ensure that your objectives are specific, measurable, attainable, relevant and time based. When you have set your objectives, you will need to measure them. Find tools to track and analyse each factor.
- Create buyer personas: Target the right people with the right messages. Understand who your audience is. Buyer personas are helpful in this regard. Create a detailed profile of your ideal customer. Give this customer a name. How old are they? What interests do they have? Where do they live?
- Research your competitors: Where on social media are your competitors active? What are they focusing on? How do they engage? Learn from your competitors.
- Develop your messages: Start building your messages. Create a unique brand voice. Be creative.
- Choose your special channels: Select the channels that are right for you. Not every social media channel is perfect for everyone. Focus on the networks that matter. Focus on your strengths and interests. Who is your target audience? For instance, LinkedIn is a good business platform.
- Build a content plan: Develop strong content that aligns with your overall message. It should be appropriate for the channels you are using. Schedule your messages and postings.

'The essence of strategy is choosing what not to do.'

MICHAEL PORTER

Summary

- ☑ A social media (marketing) strategy is about more than just posting.

- ☑ Be sure you fully understand the outcome to want from your efforts.

- ☑ When you know what you want, follow your chosen plan.

PROMOTE YOUR BRAND

THERE IS NOTHING FALSE ABOUT PROMOTING YOURSELF

Having a strong personal brand won't mean much if no one can see what you are offering. Spreading the word could be the most important element of your personal brand. Don't worry that promoting yourself will make you appear arrogant. For your promotional efforts to be effective, it would be a mistake to present yourself as overly humble. Concealing your true personality will give your promotion no chance of success.

Playing yourself down and staying small won't help you achieve success. Holding yourself back from growth and opportunities will be frustrating, and keep you from reaching your goals. Why play it small when it comes to promoting yourself and going after what you want? Are you waiting for chances to come to you instead? Stop playing it small.

There is nothing false about promoting your brand in a decent way. Here are a few suggestions for promoting your personal brand:

- Create content to demonstrate thought leadership: Create quality content that supports the way you are trying to position yourself, and that contains a distinct point of view. Make your content shareable.
- Use guest blogging: A good way to promote yourself is through guest blogging. Find sites and content that your ideal clients or audience would go to and read.
- Network, network, network: Building the right relationships is critical in promoting yourself. Going to networking events relevant to your industry offers opportunities. Or join online groups with like-minded people. Engage with people and start conversations.
- Be your own publicist: Being featured in the media is one of the best ways to become noticed in a serious way. Being featured in the press will also help position you as the go-to person in your industry. Share your expertise in articles, and send them to print publications or online magazines. Engage with journalists on social media or contact them directly when you have important news about your company. Send them your new book and chances are that they will think of you when they need a good story. Give interviews in the media.
- Join conversations: Be consistent about adding value to relevant topics on social media. Be part of conversations and demonstrate your expertise. Answer people's questions, share your opinion, comment on their content. Actively monitor

certain keywords that people are using in online conversations. These keywords should relate to your own positioning.

- Support people: You can promote your brand by supporting other people and adding value to their lives. Ask yourself how you can add value to a particular person's life.
- Share your accomplishments: There is nothing false about sharing what you have achieved. But take care that it doesn't come across as bragging. Follow these tips and you will be fine:
  - Stick to the facts
  - Keep the emphasis on the hard work you've done
  - Give credit where it's due
  - Express gratitude for what you have achieved
  - Avoid being a modest show-off
  - Don't compare yourself to other people
  - Don't belittle other people
  - Own your successes without arrogance
- Ask for testimonials and reviews: After doing a good job for a client, ask them to write a testimonial or review that you can share on social media or your website. Recommendations lead to brand trust.
- Promote your brand with photos: Instagram is a great platform for sharing photos of your brand. Share your life, work and successes. Engage with your fans and followers.
- Build brand advocates: Brand advocates can help promote your business by adding positivity to your brand and encouraging engagement by potential customers. Brand advocates are a business's most loyal, engaged and enthusiastic customers, and are likely to recommend trusted brands, products or services to their friends and community. Social media provides an easy way for brand advocates to share recommendations and reviews.

Well-known people often became well known because they showcased themselves, usually in multiple ways. They shared stories and ideas about their work; indeed, people know about their work because they know how to promote it. Promoting your work does not mean proclaiming how good you are. It does not mean puffing up your résumé. Promoting is not about presenting yourself as something you are not. It's not about shoehorning your way into other people's consciousness and telling them how great you are.

Promoting yourself in a positive way means letting a wider audience know what you have achieved until now, and doing that in a dignified, authentic and appropriate way.

People judge others by what they have achieved. Henry Wadsworth Longfellow, American poet and educator, said: 'We judge ourselves by what we feel capable of doing, while others judge us by what we have already done.'

> *'Without promotion, something*
> *terrible happens … nothing.'*
>
> **PT BARNUM**

Summary

- ☑ Branding is a long, arduous process.
- ☑ It is necessary for you to get your name out there.
- ☑ There is nothing false about promoting your brand in a responsible way.

WRITE A BOOK

BECOMING AN AUTHOR WILL HIGHLIGHT YOUR BRAND

If you want to do a bit more to showcase your brand, consider writing a book in your field. Yes, it takes a lot of work, but writing a book and expressing the thoughts inside you is worth the effort. It could be the highlight for your personal brand, writing your personal book. Is there a book inside you that should be expressed? Self-publishing has come a long way, and it is easier than ever to write and publish a quality, affordable book that will shine a light on your brand. All you need to do is create the market for your book.

Several good reasons why you should write a book:

- Establish yourself as an expert in your field
- Become a thought leader

- Become a professional speaker in your field
- Leave a legacy
- Satisfy your need to commit something to paper
- Create your personal brand
- Increase your reputation
- Stand out in the market
- Get attention and raise your visibility
- Gain authority and credibility
- Help people find you
- Encourage people to talk about you
- Launch a coaching/consulting company
- Help sell a physical product
- Help sell software
- Launch workshops/training sessions
- Draw clients to you
- Increase your reach

However, a book will not necessarily mean that you make a lot of money and become wealthy. If this is your goal in writing your book, you are on the wood path. Before writing your book, be clear about your motives. There are many ways to get attention, but writing and publishing a book is one of the best, and is an option that is generally under-utilised by entrepreneurs.

James Altucher, American hedge-fund manager, entrepreneur, venture capitalist, podcaster and bestselling author, says, 'Every entrepreneur should self-publish a book because having a book is the new business card.'

'If a story is in you, it has got to come out.'

SIMPLYBE AGENCY

Summary

☑ Seize your chance and write your book; you could profit from it in many ways.

☑ A book could be the highlight of your personal brand.

CONSISTENCY IS THE KEY TO SUCCESS

CONSISTENCY WILL FORM YOUR IDENTITY IN PEOPLE'S MINDS

Many people make consistency dependent on results and quit their projects before they know what the results will be. It pays to remember that what matters is what you do on a regular basis, consistently. Be consistent and the results will come. The way your brand looks, behaves, sounds, tastes and smells on a consistent basis forms an identity in people's minds.

Consistency is more important than our behaviour. Brand identity is built through consistency and repetition. With consistency, people will begin to trust your brand. Consistency even beats cleverness when it comes to brand success.

Of course, there's no doubt that a brand should be 'intelligent', but when people need to choose between consistency, recognition or intelligence, they usually opt for the former.

What does this mean? Once you get your brand identity right, stick with it.

'Trust is built with consistency.'

LINCOLN CHAFEE

Summary

☑ Consistency will lead to trust in your brand.

☑ Consistency will form an identity in people's minds.

☑ Learn to act consistently; it is the key to success.

116

KEY QUALITY 8: CREATE CHANCES + OPPORTUNITIES/ GET ORDERS EASILY

MAKE GREAT OPPORTUNITIES HAPPEN

We all know people who walk right into the perfect job and achieve the right promotions as though they are blessed by a special fate. They are awarded the best projects, and their presentations are acknowledged with standing ovations. How do they do it? Let's be clear: such opportunities are not down to fate, and these people don't have special genes. People who profit from consistent success know what it takes to make great opportunities happen. Great leaders know how to create chances.

All you need to do is change some habits and you will wonder why you're suddenly getting so many opportunities, too.

Do you believe in luck? Which of these proposals applies to you:

- I don't believe in luck.
- I believe that luck exists.
- I think luck is controllable.

I personally believe that luck is often the simple result of being in the right place at the right time, and you can create luck for yourself, and your company, by finding ways to put yourself in the right place at the right time. Creating your own luck begins by learning how to identify and find opportunities, but you may need to push yourself beyond your comfort zone to capitalise on them, especially if your business is in the early stages.

What you need to know when creating your own luck is that people buy from people they know, like and trust. That can be very well transferred onto relationships and chances. When people trust you, usually they will give you a chance. (There may be occasions when people demonstrate a leap of faith in you, but that seldom happens.)

You also need to learn to engage with your environment. Be curious and collect information. Reach out to people, even if a contact has no real connection to you. Be open-minded and interested in what other people have to offer. Learn to trust in serendipity. Notice things that happen around you.

See your work as important. Be proud and passionate. Honour the work you do. And be aware of your potential to make an impact. Everything you do has an impact: your smile, the way you look, and the way you talk. And your decisions affect other people, too. Learn to consider how your actions affect others around you.

Be prepared to see opportunities everywhere. Opportunity is always present. Look for ideas and trends that match your interests and your skills. And learn how to be a magnet for the jobs you do well. Offer your help and counsel willingly. When people help you, try to help them in return. Talk about your favourite projects. Let people know how much you love doing what you do well.

Count and record the opportunities that you feel will suit you. People will notice what you record and begin looking for more opportunities. Act consistently. If you consistently generate and sustain trust, you can create your own opportunities. The formula for success: TRUST + CONSISTENCY = OPPORTUNITY.

Don't hesitate when you see an opportunity. Take it and use it to grow the skills you need. Learn to grow into a position if you're not quite there yet. Develop the habit of taking on new opportunities as a way of growing. Life is about learning. Steadily.

And learn from Mark Cuban, who said so well: 'Focus on building the best possible business. If you are great, people will notice and opportunities will appear.'

You are the master of your own luck. You have the steering wheel in your hand. You can make great opportunities happen. Be versatile, open and interested, and hungry to become an expert in new areas. Once you start, you might be surprised at who pitches in to help you.

And very important: there is a world of difference between 'speaking in' requests and 'speaking in' opportunities. One of the keys to success for aspiring entrepreneurs is to learn to 'speak in' opportunities.

Don't fall into the trap and say to a good business contact, 'I need an expert for my forthcoming book who, in a few sentences, will give valuable advice on a certain topic.' Instead, say to that person: 'I would like to give you the opportunity to be seen as expert in my upcoming book. Would that be of interest to you?'

See the difference? The key here is the viewpoint: in the first example, you are seeking something; in the second, you are offering something.

'Success is where preparation and opportunity meet.'

BOBBY UNSER

Summary

☑ The 8th Key Quality of a Key Person of Trust is creating chances and opportunities, and getting orders easily.

☑ Great leaders know how to make opportunities by creating their own luck.

☑ Put yourself in a state of constant preparedness for opportunities.

☑ Be ready to act when chances come your way.

☑ Learn to 'speak in' opportunities rather than requests.

117

INCREASE
YOUR CHANCE
INTELLIGENCE (CQ)

SURROUND YOURSELF WITH
INTERESTING PEOPLE

Surround yourself with interesting people, especially those who work in different fields and see the world differently from you. If you constantly surround yourself with the same people, you risk remaining uninspired and dull. In one environment, someone may be a big fish in a small pond; in another environment they are a big fish in a small pond. Who you are and what you can do in one environment is very different from who you are and what you can do in another.

A few ideas for inspiration:

- Look over the edge of your own plate from time to time and see what others are doing.
- Make the opportunity to ask people in other fields for their opinions. Let yourself be inspired.
- Learn from different sources, including but not limited to the internet, books, magazines and webinars. Stay flexible. If you don't have the right soil you won't be able to grow.

Increase your chance intelligence (CQ). Chance intelligence means three things: 1) being able to realise chances, 2) being able to leverage those opportunities, and 3) most importantly, to actively work out chances. CQ requires focus.

'Don't join an easy crowd; you won't grow. Go where the expectations and the demands to perform are high.'

JIM ROHN

Summary

- ☑ Seek inspiration by surrounding yourself with interesting people who are different, who work in other fields.
- ☑ Learn from a variety of different sources.
- ☑ Increase your chance intelligence (CQ).

FIND THE HIDDEN VALUE IN YOUR NETWORK

THE VALUE OF DORMANT TIES

You may have heard about the concept of strong and weak ties in a network. If you needed help whom would you turn to? My bet is that you would go to one of your strongest ties. You would ask someone you know well and truly trust. Whether you were looking for a good advice or a job, it would make sense to contact one of your closest friends, family members, or colleagues.

Strong ties are those people we can trust. They understand our situation and have our best interests at heart. There is just one problem with this. Our closest contacts tend to know the same people and have the same information that we do. This is where the value of weak ties comes in.

Too often, we rely on strong ties and overlook the advantage of weak ties. Weak ties (people) are in different circles, and learn different things. This means they offer us more efficient access to novel information. In the case of job searches, for example, weak ties can be an advantage.

We have covered strong ties and weak ties. There is also a third kind of contact: dormant ties. Dormant ties are the people we used to know, those with whom we may have lost contact. Dormant ties can be the most useful of all. In general, people receive more valuable solutions, referrals, and problem-solving assistance from people they used to know than from their current friends and acquaintances. Dormant ties offer new information. During the years of no contact they have become connected to new people and have gathered new knowledge.

In summary, dormant ties combine the benefits of both strong ties and weak ties. So reach out to people you haven't seen for years when you have problems or need help and advice. Call on these people to provide you the right blend of trust and novel information. And here is a good idea: why not reconnect with at least one dormant tie each month?

'Everything you want in life is a relationship away.'

IDOWU KOYENIKAN, *WEALTH FOR ALL: LIVING A LIFE OF SUCCESS AT THE EDGE OF YOUR ABILITY*

Summary

☑ Utilise the power of your network.

☑ Reach out not only to strong and weak ties but also use the advantage of dormant ties.

☑ Dormant ties combine the benefits of strong and weak ties.

119

THE AIM OF MARKETING IS TO MAKE SELLING SUPERFLUOUS

CLIENTS SHOULD CHASE YOU

How do you get people to line up to do business with you? How do you get people to buy your products or service? On the back of Daniel Priestley's book *Oversubscribed* are these words: 'We would all love to be so highly in demand that clients chase us.' You might think that it's not possible for people not to chase clients, and instead have the reverse happen. How could demand be bigger than supply? How could people want something that much?

Here are a few inspiring suggestions for you:

- Act as if: It's important that you know what you bring to the table, that you know your stuff. When you act as if you are anticipating events in a positive way, and seeing the world differently. This will help you achieve what you want.

  Acting as if is a good tactic and attitude for even a novice entrepreneur. It allows you to overcome challenges and obstacles. Actors use this principle to begin the process of filling in a multi-layered understanding of a character. Acting as if will allow you to use your imagination and life experiences to inhabit 'disclosive spaces' as part of your journey to achieve your goals. A disclosive space is the way each of us sees the world and operates in it—our personal perspective—and our way of understanding how different complexities are interrelated, and how we fit into them.

  The technique will also give you the opportunity to become the person you imagine yourself to be. It can make you feel small, but it can also make you feel big. Learn to act as if and achieve the success you want.

- Be a campaign-driven enterprise (CDE): Learn to differentiate your company and yourself from other companies and people. Are you running a business or a CDE? It's important that you identify your business as a CDE. This approach will provide you with the right strategic mindset to focus on running powerful campaigns. When you adopt this identity, you will become oversubscribed and clients will chase you.

  Daniel Priestley explains: 'I have never gone out to get one customer at a time. I run events and promotions that encourage everyone to come to us all at once. I want people to feel a buzz and an excitement. Sitting with one potential customer at a time kills the energy for me, the team, and the clients. Every entrepreneur, leader or marketing manager must learn how to encourage ten, twenty or even hundreds of people at one time to engage with their business.'

- Learn to improvise: What do you do when you are faced with difficulties? Life is not perfect, and we never know what's around the corner. Improvisation can help. Improvisation can be learned. For example, if technology stopped working overnight we would all be helpless. In this situation, we would profit from seizing the opportunity to overcome the difficult situation by having the best attitude.

  Improvisation can help you with your performance during speeches and other events. It can give you trust in yourself, and the confidence to stay calm. Improvisation means having the right spontaneous and flexible reaction for unexpected moments in business. It can help prevent insecurity and tragedies.

- Make selling superfluous: Peter Drucker, writer, professor, management consultant and self-described social-ecologist, widely known as the father of management, said: 'The customer rarely buys what the business thinks it sells him. One reason for this is, of course, that nobody pays for a "product". What is paid for is satisfaction. But nobody can make or supply satisfaction, as such—at best, only the means to attaining them can be sold and delivered.' Customers should know you have their best interests at heart, and place real value on the offers you make.

'There will always, one can assume, be need for some selling. But the aim of marketing is to make selling superfluous. The aim of marketing is to know and understand the customer so well that the product or service fits him and sells itself.'

PETER DRUCKER, *MANAGEMENT*

Summary

☑ Learn to act as if.

☑ Don't chase clients; instead, let them chase you.

☑ Be a campaign-driven enterprise.

☑ Learn to improvise your way through difficulties to success.

☑ Understand your customer well enough to make selling superfluous.

BUILD EFFECTIVE CUSTOMER RELATIONSHIPS

STRONG RELATIONSHIPS ARE CRITICAL FOR BUSINESS SUCCESS

Do you stand out in today's business world? Why should customers choose your business over another? Building effective customer relationships is critical for your business success, but that doesn't mean you have to become friends with your customers. Don't take to heart this quote by JC Penney: 'Every great business is built on friendship.' Instead, take note of this one by Katherine Barchetti: 'Make a customer, not a sale.'

Here are some tips for building your customer relationships:

- Show an interest in your customers: Listen to them, and remember their background stories, preferences and concerns. Understand their goals and needs. Damon Richards says: 'Your customer doesn't care how much you know until they know how much you care.'
- Offer educational content: Create personal messages, offers and rewards based on your customers' needs; this will add value.
- Support your customers' businesses: Learn about your customers' businesses, and support them. Exchange business cards; your customers will appreciate referrals.
- Ask for feedback: If you have a new product or service, ask potential customers for their opinions.
- Deliver excellent customer service: Always do more than necessary. Send long-time customers free products or discounts.

'There are no traffic jams along the extra mile.'

ROGER STAUBACH

Summary

☑ When you exceed expectations you increase customer satisfaction and loyalty.

☑ Keep your customers happy, build trust in your business, and strengthen customer relationships.

GETTING CUSTOMERS: RESIST THE URGE TO MAKE IT WORK

NOT EVERY CUSTOMER IS A GOOD FIT

Every business owner wants a consistent flow of qualified prospects and customers. Without a constant flow of sales meetings you won't have a fast-growth company. Think of the word 'prospecting' in the sense of prospecting for gold; the goal is not to find copper and try to convert it to gold, but to find the precious metal itself.

Too often we look for our salvation in possibilities. We pretend a bad prospect might become a good customer, but the reality is, bad is always bad. It is either gold or it is not. If it isn't gold, we should forget about it and move on.

It is a mistake to try to make things work by taking on clients that aren't a perfect fit simply because you don't want to give up the chance of getting an order. Companies make this mistake all the time. Resist the urge to make it work when it comes to getting customers, because this approach only leads to dissatisfied customers and bad testimonials. And you can also damage your reputation, and affect customer attrition and your profit.

You're better off looking for a new prospect. Alternatively, you could find out if the prospect's need could be met with another product or service that you offer. The best scenario is that you develop your business to the point where customers find you, rather than you having to chase customers.

*'A satisfied customer is the best
business strategy of all.'*

MICHAEL LEBOEUF

Summary

☑ Resist the urge to make your customers fit your business.

☑ Not every prospect will be a good fit.

☑ It is better to concentrate on prospects that are easy to handle.

☑ Consider developing your business so that customers can find you.

CONCENTRATE ON YOUR IDEAL CUSTOMERS

DEFINING THE PERFECT CUSTOMER

Not all customers are the perfect fit; indeed, some can be difficult and I'm sure you prefer customers who are easy to work with. Customers who are not easy to work with can bring trouble, complicate communication and delay the sales process. Learn to concentrate on the perfect customers for your business. How do you find them? Many people struggle with this question. When it comes to figuring out who their ideal customers are, many entrepreneurs get stuck. They might have a vague idea of who their target group is, or who they want to serve, but they haven't yet done the work to get it right.

Accept that you can't serve everyone, at least not very well. But making connections with the right people can supercharge your business growth. The perfect customers for your business will meet the following criteria:

- Have a similar worldview, and share your values and beliefs
- Have a problem that you can solve.
- Can afford you (tip: double your prices today)
- Are willing to engage with you

Connecting with the right customers is an amazing experience. When you do, powerful things will follow. You'll find they are easy to communicate with, they will gladly pay for your services and products, they will recommend you, and they will become loyal to your brand. Isn't that nice? Yes, it is.

To find your ideal customer, you could start by looking at groups on social media (e.g. Facebook, LinkedIn.) Think about your ideal customer. What do they look like? What do you like most about your imagined ideal customer? Can you visualise them? What problems could you help your ideal customer solve?

When your business has become so attractive to your target customers that they buy from you, you will have become successful.

*'It is not about accepting who you find
but choosing who to attract.'*

KARIN SEBELIN

Summary

☑ Don't run after every possible customer.

☑ Learn how to find the ideal customers for your business.

☑ Make your business so attractive that customers chase you.

LOVE THE CUSTOMERS WHO ARE NOT 'NORMAL'

EXPAND YOUR RANGE OF POTENTIAL CUSTOMERS

The business owner who focuses only on 'normal' clients stays mainstream and misses opportunities. Mainstream reflects the taste of the majority. Nothing is easier than courting 'normal' clients; instead, look for clients who are not normal.

Stefan Sagmeister, Austrian graphic designer and typographer, says: 'I only work with clients that are smarter than me.' You may have become accustomed to appreciating those clients who regularly ask for large quantities, don't make a big effort, don't know the words 'special wishes', and pay their bills on time. Your offers are always the same, don't differ much from the competition, and everything is interchangeable and arbitrary. If this is you, you might be sinking into the ocean of normality.

The customers who will really help you are those who catapult you out of your comfort zone. Ever tried to 'press' clients with unusual wishes in a normal scheme? Forget it. Don't overlook the value of taking care of clients who don't fit the description of a normal customer.

> *'Your most unhappy customers are*
> *your greatest source of learning.'*

BILL GATES

Summary

☑ Avoid overdependence on normal clients.

☑ Look for and appreciate clients who are not 'normal'.

CONSUMERS BUY WHAT THEY WANT, NOT WHAT THEY NEED

WHAT THE CONSUMER BELIEVES IS ALL THAT MATTERS

People pay extra for eggs that are marketed as being antibiotic free. You could argue that *all* egg-laying chickens are raised without antibiotics. That may be true, but in this case the facts are irrelevant. All that matters is what the consumer believes. And they really believe in buying antibiotic-free eggs. In former times, making a product or service better or cheaper than another was a sure path to growth and success, but the rules have changed. Consumers now buy what they want, not what they need. The path to profitable growth and success is in satisfying wants, and not needs.

'Business is all about the customer: what the customer wants and what they get.'

FABRIZIO MOREIRA

Summary

☑ Try to satisfy wants, not needs, in order to become successful.

CREATING LOYAL CUSTOMERS

BUILDING LIFELONG CUSTOMER RELATIONSHIPS

One option for creating more chances and opportunities is by focusing on relationship marketing. The term 'relationship marketing' was first introduced in 1986 by Dr Leonard L Berry, who defined it as attracting, maintaining and enhancing customer relationships. Several themes in the current literature emphasise customer satisfaction, mutual trust and commitment or promise. There is a perspective that compares marketing relationships with marriage, with mutual commitment and interest of both parties. Another perspective states that relationship marketing is an asymmetrical process that requires a deep and personalised understanding of customer needs and characteristics.

Whatever the perspective, the aim of relationship marketing is simply to create loyalty in all customers.

Here is a good definition of relationship marketing: those efforts that will make your prospects aware of your products and services, position your business as the obvious choice, and help build lifelong and profitable customer relationships. Relationship marketing, above all, means caring about all people and building solid relationships where all parties profit. This means relationships with your prospects, clients, key influencers, media contacts, and even your competitors.

People have always done business with people they know, like and trust. That is the essence of relationship marketing.

> *'Relationships are like muscle tissue. The more they're engaged, the stronger they become. The ability to build relationships and flex that emotional connection muscle is what makes social so valuable.'*

TED RUBIN

Summary

☑ The focus and the aim of relationship marketing is to move all customers towards more loyalty.

KEY QUALITY 9: GOOD REPUTATION

REPUTATION IS WHAT PEOPLE SAY ABOUT YOU

Reputation is very important; you want both you and your business to been seen in the best possible light. Prospects and customers who are looking for the best business to deal with make their choice based on the person and company that appear to be superior. You may say, but I have good character so that's not a problem. But that's not the full story.

Character is indeed very important, but in the end it is about reputation. It begins with good character, but you should aim for a good reputation. The difference between character and reputation: your character is what you are actually like; your reputation is what other people think you are like. Character is objective; reputation is subjective. Reputation is all about perception.

You have probably heard these words several times in your life: 'It doesn't matter what others think of you, but only what you think of yourself.' This is the easiest advice to give—and it is completely false. What others think of you is *always* important. A positive reputation is critical if you want to be successful. You may not be able to control what others think of you, but you can very well influence your reputation.

For a start, the way you speak and act determines, to a large extent, what others think of you. You may think that you are a cool, calm and collected person, but if you are not giving that impression then other people will not perceive those qualities in you. Be aware that every action you take affects your reputation. Other people notice how you communicate and how you act. Everything you do and say is a reflection of you. Your name is attached to everything you communicate, whether spoken or written. You owe it to yourself and to your business to behave in an appropriate way. Your reputation, both on- and offline, is perhaps one of the most powerful marketing tools you have at your disposal.

In the world today, our reputation—the way others perceive us—exists both in real life and online. Everyone, from teenager to entrepreneur, has a reputation, regardless of whether it is good, bad or somewhere in between. We are experiencing a fundamental paradigm shift from the 'information age' towards the 'reputation age', where information will have value only if it has already been filtered, evaluated and commented upon by others. Not just a central pillar of collective intelligence, reputation is now the gatekeeper to knowledge.

'A good reputation is more valuable than money.'

PUBLILIUS SYRUS

Summary

☑ The 9th Key Quality of a Key Person of Trust is having a good reputation.

☑ Character is not the same thing as reputation: character is what you are; reputation is what people say you are.

YOUR REPUTATION DEPENDS ON WHAT YOU HAVE DONE

PLANS ARE JUST A MEANS TO AN END

Your reputation depends who you are perceived to be, and how you show up, day after day. If you want to build a good reputation, you need to take (massive) action. A good reputation does not come from planning alone; it requires that you take concrete action.

It is easy to invest in planning and forget to act. Plans are wonderful, and necessary for success, but without the necessary fulfilment you will have no success. When people see what you are able to achieve they will respect and appreciate your work, and that in turn will increase your reputation. In business, we are all ultimately measured by what we have done.

*'You can't build a reputation on
what you are going to do.'*

HENRY FORD

Summary

☑ Make plans a reality and show the
world what you want to achieve.

☑ Reputation is measured by what you
have done.

BUILD A STRONG BUSINESS REPUTATION

LEARN TO MANAGE YOUR REPUTATION

What is involved in building a good reputation? According to the Davies and Miles corporate reputation review, titled 'Reputation Management: Theory versus Practice', reputation as it pertains to business involves three things:

1. How others see your business
2. Who the business really is
3. What the business communicates about itself

When managing your business reputation, you must align these three elements. Even if only one element is out of balance, your entire reputation can come crashing down. The following factors shape a business reputation:

- Visual cues: name, logo, all of the imagery related to the company
- Mission, vision and philosophy (the guiding light of a company's internal culture)
- Behaviour of people within the organisation: word of mouth, news, articles
- Success of the business

Your reputation decides your future opportunities. A great reputation may lead to opportunities presenting themselves when they are least expected.

So how do you create a positive reputation for your business? Creating, curating and maintaining a positive reputation for a business is certainly no easy task, but it will help if you remember one of the most important factors regarding human psychology: consistency. According to a US news article, traits like honesty, kindness and generosity help to foster a good reputation in the workplace. Group-oriented behaviours also pay dividends when it comes to bolstering a business's reputation.

One thing to remember: if you are on social media you are always networking. Don't assume that any statement or post is going to go unnoticed. Maintaining a positive reputation that aligns with who you are is critical, so always try to leave a good (first) impression. Know how you want to be perceived. Act with consistency. Your intentions behind any action you make should match the results. Develop a sense of how others perceive you.

A few helpful recommendations for establishing a good reputation:

- Blog frequently, keeping your content fresh and original
- Create landing pages
- Write guest posts
- Establish a podcast
- Publish press releases
- Publish case studies, e-books and guides that relate to your business
- Develop infographics and lists
- Undertake interviews with industry leaders
- Ramp up your content-marketing operation
- Invest in great 'old-fashioned' customer service, which means going the extra mile for your customers and learning to appreciate every contact

And now a few things to avoid if you don't want to destroy an already good reputation:

- Copying other people's content; take note of copyright laws
- Overemphasising your knowledge
- Talking about subjects where you are no expert and insisting on your opinion
- Overreacting to personal attacks
- Not being transparent about upcoming problems

What is your current reputation based on? Is it based on exams, certificates, graduations or position in a company? Does it depend on content that you stand for? Or is it based on an established and well-known own brand? To answer this question, it might be helpful to do the following:

- Create a list with two to three adjectives describing how you want to be perceived.
- Ask good friends and contacts how they perceive you.
- Before you leave the house each morning look in the mirror. (What kind of first impression do you think you make?)
- Decide on three action steps to grow your personal brand and act consistently.
- Check your social media profiles. (Are they aligned with your personal brand? Use them to promote a positive reputation.)

'It takes twenty years to build a reputation and five minutes to ruin it. If you think about that, you'll do things differently.'

WARREN BUFFET

Summary

☑ Your reputation is based on how the world views you, so act accordingly.

☑ Invest in your reputation.

GOOGLE YOURSELF

SEARCH FOR YOURSELF ONLINE

I t's to your advantage to take an interest in what is written about you on the internet. There could be information about you that gives a false impression or affects your reputation adversely. When people look for your name, they could find false, bad or inappropriate information. What you find on Google about you can be critical for your success, and needs to be taken seriously.

Use quotation marks around your name when you do a search on Google so you get results with that exact phrase. Don't stop with the first page of results. Scroll through every page that mentions you. If you find something that's incorrect, contact the site administrator or Google and request that it is removed. In difficult cases, you may need to involve a lawyer.

'Google is arguably one of the greatest inventions. The search engine is one of the greatest inventions in human history.'

FRANKLIN FOER

Summary

☑ Search for yourself on Google and take steps if your reputation could be adversely affected.

130

KEY QUALITY 10: MORE TRUST + MORE INFLUENCE

TRUST IS A NECESSITY AND INFLUENCE IS AN ART

Influence is being able to affect actions. Influence is the key to success. If you are able to inspire or change people's behaviour, that means you have influence. A brand is a name with the power to influence. Manipulation, persuasion and coercion are all words that are commonly used to mean influence:

- Manipulation: In this example, the meaning of influence has a negative connotation. Manipulation is characterised by efforts to try and change someone's beliefs by any means.

- Persuasion: This means convincing someone to buy based on an offer, or offering the best solution to someone's problems. Persuasion is about trying to change someone's belief.
- Coercion: The meaning here is to focus on changing someone's behaviour, often through verbal or even physical violence (robbery, blackmail and many other crimes fit this category).

If you're not sure whether you're dealing with a case of manipulation, persuasion or coercion, ask yourself two questions: Is this person trying to benefit at my expense? Is this person trying to change my beliefs or my behaviour?

We can be clear about one thing: influence is not about trying to change people's beliefs. Rather, influence means trying to get someone to change their behaviour to the benefit of someone.

There are four criteria related to the concept of influence:

1. Trust: Trust is the conduit for influence. Trust is the medium through which ideas travel. When people don't trust you, your ideas will not benefit you. When they do trust you, they will listen to you. The more trust people have in you, the higher your influence. That's why influence is so difficult to obtain; you have to earn the trust, commitment and support of other people.

   The problem is that other people's priorities will not always be the same as yours. People often have their own strongly held beliefs and principles, and think and behave very differently than you do. As a businessperson and marketer, you must establish a level of trust with your prospects and customers, and create a belief that your product or services are a good fit for them.

2. Authority: Authority means that you have established some expertise; you have given people a good reason to believe in what you are saying. You have established a certain level of 'I know what I am talking about' or 'I am an expert in my field'.
3. Benefit: Why should people believe you? What benefit will they get if they buy your products and services? Give people a reason to follow and believe in you.
4. Connection: Establish some kind of connection with the people you want to influence. Think about who influences you; think about your relationships with them.

The ability to influence other people is one of the essential skills for a leader. It's not that easy to influence people. In fact, it's more art than science. Influence is the process of taking your own perception of the truth and passing it onto others. The problem is that each of us has their own idea of what the truth is. Influence matters, and as we continue to work online, it will only matter more.

'Be the person that people know like and trust. Develop your influence further.'

KARIN SEBELIN

Summary

☑ The 10th Key Quality of a Key Person of Trust is enjoying more trust and more influence.

☑ The only way you can influence people is through your ability to relate to them. And if you want to relate to people, the only way that's going to happen is through trust.

☑ The more trust you can develop, the more you can relate to, influence and lead other people.

UNDERSTAND YOUR STYLE OF INFLUENCE

HOW TO BECOME AN EFFECTIVE INFLUENCER

To influence means to induce beliefs, attitudes, values and behaviours in other people by influencing their thoughts and actions through specific strategies. When was the last time you thought about your own influence? How do you influence others (change minds, affect hearts, shape opinions and move people to act)? To become an effective influencer, you need both substance and style. We have discussed substance already as part of the 2nd Key Quality. Let's talk about style now. To be successful, you need to understand your style of leadership and influence.

In 2009 and 2010, Discovery Learning Inc. and Innovative Pathways conducted research to identify and measure different influence styles. The result was five categories of influence styles, each of which can be effective depending on the situation and the people involved:

1. Asserting: leaders insist that their own ideas are heard and they challenge others' ideas
2. Convincing: Leaders put forward their own ideas and offer logical arguments to convince others
3. Negotiating: leaders look for compromises and make concessions
4. Bridging: leaders build relationships and connect with others
5. Inspiring: leaders advocate their own position and encourage others with a sense of shared purpose and exciting possibilities

How can you increase your own influence? First you need to become aware of your individual influencing style. Which style from the research most closely matches your own, asserting, convincing, negotiating, bridging or inspiring? To help you decide, I suggest you use the Influence Style Indicator by Discovery Learning. The Influence Style Indicator is an assessment instrument designed to understand an individual's preferred style as they influence others. The assessment addresses one's preferred, secondary and underutilised influencing styles. Discovery Learning International (DLI) is now part of Multi-Health Systems Inc. (MHS) and you will find the link to the Influence Style Indicator at www.mhs.com/MHS-DLI1?prodname=isi.

Be clear about your own situation. Who are the critical people you need to win over? Identify any gaps. This means figuring out where you are on solid ground and where you need a different approach. When you have the answer, develop yourself further in those areas, either through workshops, coaching or a mentor. And then practise. Begin with small steps and test your new influencing approaches, and see what works and what doesn't.

'The key to successful leadership today is influence, not authority.'

KEN BLANCHARD

Summary

☑ To become successful with regard to influence, determine your own influence style and develop yourself further.

THE ART OF PERSUASION

USING ARISTOTLE'S THREE MEANS OF PERSUASION

nfluence is about persuasion. Only when you are able to persuade others will you have influence. Persuasion is a powerful ability, and you should use it to your advantage. Knowledge about persuasion is ancient; even Aristotle wrote about it and its principles. According to Aristotle, persuasion can be broken down into three components: ethos (character), pathos (passion) and logos (reasoning).

1. Ethos: Ethos is the appeal to character or reputation. To persuade others, you need to establish credibility and authority with your audience. This makes you trustworthy. People will decide within

minutes whether to trust you or not. Are you honest? Do you demonstrate integrity?

Ethos means appearing knowledgeable about the topic you are speaking about and being a person of good character. Are you qualified to be an expert in your area? You could use ethos in many ways. You could begin your speech or text by referring to your expertise in the subject. Or you could try to find common ground with your audience, since human beings have a tendency to trust others who are similar to them.

Living a life of virtue is perhaps the best way to develop ethos. When you come over as virtuous, honest and earnestly committed, your audience will love you.

2. Pathos: Pathos is the appeal to emotion, the passion you have for your subject. In order for others to believe in you, you first need to believe in yourself. Some people have a tendency to dismiss the power of emotion. They would rather use reason and logic. However, in a battle between emotion and rationality, emotion usually wins because humans are emotional creatures. People are more likely to remember stories than facts because stories tap into the emotions. So try to use the power of emotion more often in presentations and meetings. Metaphors can be a good tool.

3. Logos: Logos is the appeal to reason, which you can use to build an objective, rational, logical and unambiguous argument. If pathos is the work of the heart then logos is the work of the head. You need logos to express goals, techniques and facts. Logical arguments based on objectivity and facts create understanding. Aristotle thought logos should be our aim and that all arguments should be won or lost on reason alone.

When selling ideas, all three of Aristotle's categories—ethos, pathos and logos— should be present. Here is an example of a person's thought process where each of the three means of persuasion was used successfully:

1.   They understand my problem very well (pathos).
2.   They have a problem just like mine (pathos).
3.   They respect my point of view (pathos).
4.   They really seem to know what they are talking about (ethos).
5.   Their solution for my problem sounds logical (logos).
6.   I will follow their advice.

'The fool tells me his reasons. The wise man persuades me with my own.'

ARISTOTLE

Summary

☑ Learning something about the three means of persuasion can help you become successful as a Key Person of Trust.

☑ Only when you are able to persuade others will you be able to influence them.

133

BUILD A NETWORK AND BECOME A CENTRE OF INFLUENCE

FORMULA FOR BUILDING A LOYAL COMMUNITY

Now we dig a bit deeper into the topic of influence. When a leader is able to lead a group in a special way, they can become a centre of influence. They can persuade or cause someone to take specific action. The larger the group, the greater the person's reach and influence can be. Some influencers are able to create a ripple effect. Can you persuade your network to take action? Can you move people to action? You want to become a centre of influence? What is a centre of influence? It's someone who is well-known, respected and trusted in the community and, as a result, has significant influence. Build a loyal community by following this formula:

- Build a network of quality: Use the right strategy and develop your online profiles with the right mix of target market, prospects, customers, peers and resources.
- Deliver quality content: Provide your audience with excellent and relevant material.
- Show consistency: Consistency is the key to success, so be sure to show up regularly.
- Be genuine, authentic, credible, passionate and caring: Demonstrate your trustworthiness through your actions.
- Help others and be a people connector: Always be on the lookout for chances to introduce your contacts to each other for their mutual interest.

'The greatest ability in business is to get along with others and to influence their actions.'

JOHN HANCOCK

☑ Build a loyal community and become recognised as a centre of influence.

Summary

134

INCREASE YOUR INFLUENCE

DEVELOP YOUR SKILLS AND TALENTS

Some people seem to be born for success. They are gifted intellectually and physically, and appear to be 'flying' to success. But don't be fooled. However gifted someone may be, they still had to do *something* to achieve their success. They had to develop their talents to achieve whatever professional position they hold.

You can take positive steps towards achieving your own success. You already have skills and talents that you can capitalise on, and by developing yourself further you can gain influence. Learn twelve ways to enhance those talents and increase your influence:

1. Think like a leader: Influence is most obvious when we lead. When you act like a leader, you think like a leader. Develop your

leadership and help others become successful. Herminia Ibarra, Paris-based Cora-chaired professor of leadership and learning at INSEAD has written a wonderful book called *Act Like a Leader, Think Like a Leader*. Herminia writes in the opening chapter of the book: 'The only way to think like a leader is to first act: to plunge yourself into new projects and activities, interact with different kinds of people, and experiment with unfamiliar ways of getting things done.'

2. Become a storyteller: Storytelling is a great tool for influencing people across cultures and in all areas. A well-told narrative is a powerful force for motivating people to act, for teaching and for changing minds. Whether you tell stories on Twitter or write interesting blogs, show what you know and learn to inspire others.

   Through stories we remember the parables and the life lessons, and we are better able to connect to a person or organisation. And it is no surprise that the businesses with the greatest loyalty, and the best relationships and subscribers are those that are in the business of storytelling. For stories to really work, to have power in the long run, they have to be honest, authentic and even human.

   Through stories we relate to people and companies. So learn to tell stories, and to write quality content and become an authority as a quality curator. A thought leader is able to express their thoughts in a way that creates more significant leadership. There is an ancient Native American proverb that says: 'Those who tell the stories rule the world.'

3. Develop your speaking skills: Don't shy away from speaking opportunities. Seize your chance and put yourself in front of an audience. Develop your abilities further. Start in smaller settings

first, and build up from there. Learn to perform. Remember: All the world's a stage.

4. Understand communication technology: We are in the 21st century, and our lives are defined by communication technology. Businesses are online, and people are looking for those in business to be present. Work on your skills to enable and enhance your influence. Developing your communication skills further and learning the newest technology will always be to your advantage.

5. Develop expertise: Another way to increase your influence is to become a recognised expert within your industry or organisation. This won't happen overnight, no question, but you can take steps to develop business-critical expertise and increase your knowledge. Visit industry conferences, sign up for courses, or take a relevant role in a professional organisation. You can educate yourself on all aspects of your job. Become visible, open and interested. Stay up to date and informed.

6. Build valuable connections: Building connections of value is key to success. At a fundamental level, it is one of the reasons people support your ideas, give you chances and work with you. Learn to cultivate personal connections and allow people to get to know you.

7. Sell your ideas and vision: Your best ideas will be useless if you don't 'sell' them. A good leader must also be a good salesman in order to garner support from prospects, customers, the community, and other leaders and team members. It's not only about 'telling' your vision, but also about 'selling' your vision. A clear vision will help your followers know exactly what to expect from you.

Explain how each individual can contribute to the overall success of the company. George Hallenbeck, contributor to the book *Lead 4 Success: Learn the Essentials of True Leadership*, says: 'Without the ability to capture the hearts, minds, and energy of others, the truly important things in work and life can't be achieved.'

8. Show courage: If you want to be successful, you should prove that you have courage. Making decisions that reveal that you have the courage and confidence to take a stand can only help.

9. Involve people: Identify the strengths and skills of other people, including team members and colleagues, and give them the chance to collaborate with you. Involve other people in your projects and meetings. Put weight on their opinions. Hear what they have to say. Delegate.

10. Help others succeed: Great leaders support others, thereby sowing seeds for success. A great leader is always a teacher, a mentor for others. They 'reproduce' other influencers by finding people with leadership potential and developing their personalities further. They give people opportunities, and empower people to make an impact.

11. Care for others: Try to understand other people and their individual needs. Leaders truly care for the people they are leading. Each individual requires a different style of management. Develop good character traits such as empathy, compassion, and respect.

12. Express sincere appreciation: The real way to win a person over is through sincere appreciation and compliments. Decide what you like about someone and tell them. Flattery might be enjoyable, but the real way to go is sincere appreciation.

'Leadership is influence.'

JOHN C MAXWELL

Summary

☑ To increase your influence, develop your skills and talents (this will take practice).

☑ Consistency is the key to your success.

☑ Influence means that your messages and body language are consistent at all times.

135

TURN INFLUENCE INTO INCOME

LEVERAGE INFLUENCE TO BUILD A PROFITABLE BUSINESS

The great thing about having influence is that you can monetise it in multiple ways. You can make money from consultations, books, speaking gigs, digital products and much more. Here five key suggestions for turning your influence into income:

1. Forget the need to be original: Originality is overrated. You don't need to come up with an original idea to become successful as influencer. The greatest thought leaders often become the 'translators' of their field. Dorie Clark, author of the book *Stand Out: How to Develop Your Breakthrough Idea and Build a Following Around It* calls these people 'synthesisers'. Such people don't

come up with a groundbreaking new idea or piece of research; instead, they bring together ideas and create a synthesis that shows their target market a new and simple way to look at what's already out there.

Here's an idea: seek out some interesting ideas that did not get the attention and coverage they deserved. Ask yourself what other people in your field are overlooking. What are they not talking about? Try to combine multiple ideas and give them a new perspective. This could become your breakthrough idea.

2. Use your background to stand out: You have a unique background, even if it's just a certain philosophical approach. It could be demographic, or a pivot away from a certain industry. This gives you a real competitive edge. It means you have a different perspective and bring unique talents to the party.

3. Get your hands dirty: Thought leaders often start out without knowing what they are interested in. They immerse themselves in their industry to see where they can insert themselves and contribute. You can do this, too. It might mean road-testing your ideas, accumulating relevant testimonials and affiliations, and becoming an expert in your field. Dorie Clark says: 'The "game" is to get as much credibility as you can early on, and then leverage that credibility so you can turn it into premium prices down the road.'

4. Break down your ideas: Too often, we rely on our skills and talent. We take them for granted. But other people who don't have those skills can profit from them. Ask people what their main interests are. Is there anything that could be a useful topic for your network?

5. Charge your price: A big challenge is having the confidence to name your own price. You might not know what to charge,

or simply throw out figures that don't do justice to your value. Here is a good recommendation by Michael Bungay Stanier, author of *The Coaching Habit*. He says that a price should always be 'Fear + 10%'. This means that you should pick the amount you are afraid to say, add 10 percent and deliver it with certainty.

> *'If you make a living, if you earn your*
> *own money, you're free—however*
> *free one can be on this planet.'*

THEODORE WHITE

Summary

☑ Once you've built your influence it's time to monetise it in multiple ways.

☑ Learning how to monetise your influence is a good way to start.

PROMOTE YOURSELF

INCREASE YOUR INFLUENCE

Self-promotion is often seen with distrustful eyes. This is because some people handle self-promotion falsely. These are people who 'drum up business', come across as braggarts or selfish. There are definitely people who fit into the category of spammers. When we constantly receive messages from the same person inviting us to the same event, without having subscribed to their news, this is a kind of spam. Severe self-promotion that puts people under pressure and goes against common courtesy does not work.

What is the difference between bragging and self-promotion? Bragging means over-emphasising your own value to relevant and irrelevant audiences in order to make yourself feel secure or superior. Self-promotion means educating relevant people in an organisation or marketplace about your skills, work and achievements, and the value you offer.

Why is self-promotion so difficult? The problem lies in the 'self' part. As human beings, we live our ego. When we hear people aggressively promoting themselves, we tune them out. Such people come over as insincere salespeople who just want to make the sale and don't care what people want or need.

Influential leaders know that by promoting themselves in an authentic way, and for the right reasons, they can cut through the masses of information that bombards us all every day. Self-promotion is a key to influencing others. It isn't just a tool to advance your own career and to sell yourself. It can provide visibility and credibility, and even opportunities. Real self-promotion is genuine and authentic, and will give people a reason to associate themselves with you; it will increase your success and brand.

Here are the main rules for using self-promotion in a positive way:

- Add value: Show your prospects and existing clients the value you offer.
- Be sensitive to context: This means being aware of whom you're talking to, and the conditions in which you're relating to them.
- Express confidence: Show that you have faith in yourself, your abilities and your work.
- Explain what you do: Outline clearly and exactly what you do and what you offer.
- Be on target: Direct your message toward those who most need or want to hear it.
- Ask permission: Make sure that people have given you permission to promote yourself.
- Respect people's time: Make sure that you don't overstrain people's time.

Some people are reluctant to blow their own horn but still want to do something in the way of self-promotion. Here are a few suggestions:

- Help other people without expecting anything in return.
- Serve people, but don't sell; instead let your actions be your sales pitch.
- Introduce others to interesting people they could benefit from.
- Give away valuable ideas for free.
- Promote talented professionals.
- Partner with other people who have solid reputations, shared key values and common goals.
- Develop true expertise in one or two areas; in other words, specialise.
- Become a valuable, reliable source of good information on special topics.
- Be proud and honest, and don't hide your achievements.
- Ask for recommendations, testimonials and referrals.

Good self-promotion needs support from others, so if you want to reach a wider audience with your self-promotion, cast a wider net. Ask for help on social media, through newsletters, etc.

'Self-promotion is not about being pushy.'

KARIN SEBELIN

Summary

☑ Learn to cut through the noise with authentic and credible self-promotion to increase your influence.

☑ Self-promotion, handled with charm and cultivated manners, can help you become successful.

☑ Be very proud of yourself and your achievements because you've earned it.

BECOME A GIVER

INFLUENTIAL PEOPLE GIVE BACK

You may know the book *Give and Take* by Adam Grant, top-rated professor at Wharton. In his book, Adam Grant demonstrates that givers in general achieve extraordinary results across a wide range of industries. Giving has a surprising impact on success. In life there are takers, matchers and givers. Takers strive to get as much as possible from connections, matchers aim to trade evenly, and givers are a rare breed who contribute to others without expecting anything in return.

To become a giver, learn to be 'other-minded'. Instead of thinking only of yourself, put others first. It might not always be easy. Only when you are at peace with yourself will you be able to be other-minded and give yourself away to others. As influencer you should learn to give something back.

The effects on other people when you become a giver:

- Feel they have self-worth
- Have a sense of belonging
- Have perspective
- Enjoy a feeling of significance
- Experience hope
- Have learned to trust you

Now you might ask how you become a giver. Even if you are not a natural giver, you can learn to become one. Anyone can become a giver and add value to others. Here's how you can become a giver:

- Make a commitment: Focus on helping people, and if necessary change your priorities and actions.
- Believe in people: Give others your trust and spread hope.
- Be accessible: Make time for other people and their problems.
- Give without expectation: Instead of trying to get something in return, give freely without expectations.
- Offer opportunities: Give people chances where possible.
- Lift people to a higher level: Help people reach their full potential.

'If you want to be a generous giver, you have to watch out for selfish takers.'

ADAM GRANT

Summary

- ☑ Try to become a giver.

- ☑ Develop a nurturing environment in your home and business, where people feel respected and secure.

- ☑ Encourage people and help them achieve success.

- ☑ Giving fosters relationships and leads to trust.

COMMUNICATE
FROM THE HEART

DEVELOP A MAKE-A-
DIFFERENCE ATTITUDE

You can connect with people and lead them only if you value them. But how can you show that you value them? First, don't take people for granted. Don't take relationships for granted. Valuing people is the first step in the connection process. Only when you value people will you be able to create trust. Trust leads to influence. When you let people know that you don't take them for granted, they will do the same for you.

As a leader, you need to possess a make-a-difference attitude. But how can you make a difference? Start by learning to communicate from the heart. Once you've initiated a connection with another person, found common ground, and discovered what matters to them, communicate from the heart. Communicate what matters to you.

Being genuine is the most important factor, as it is ensuring that you are not simply playing a role. No amount of knowledge, quick-wittedness or technology can substitute for honesty and the genuine desire to support others. So, as you communicate with others in order to build connections, share from your heart and be authentic.

> *'The best and most beautiful things in the world cannot be seen or even touched, they must be felt with the heart.'*

HELEN KELLER

Summary

- ☑ Learn to communicate from the heart.
- ☑ Share what it is important to you, what moves you and what interests you.
- ☑ Communicating from the heart creates valuable connections, leads to trust and increases influence.
- ☑ Develop a make-a-difference attitude.

Bonus Material

Rules for Trust

Trust Rule No 1: We cannot completely control whether people trust us. It depends not only on us, but also the person themselves.

Trust Rule No 2: Trust is not a random product, but a relationship quality that we can systematically build, strengthen and foster.

Trust Rule No 3: Trust represents innocence. Everything can be taken from a human being except their innocence, trust, human dignity and soul.

Trust Rule No 4: Distrust is contrary to trust. It gives our counterpart bad feelings and makes them distrustful toward us. Distrust impairs, from the beginning, the relationship between two people. Trust and control don't fit together.

Trust Rule No 5: Rivalry impairs trust and engenders suspicion. Jealousy and envy are counterproductive to building trust.

Trust Rule No 6: First impressions do count, but they can be deceiving. We should avoid making snap judgements about other people.

Trust Rule No 7: Giving other people our trust without caution can backfire.

Trust Rule No 8: The risk with trust is that it make us vulnerable. We should be aware that we can get hurt.

Trust Rule No 9: Mutual trust means that we have an interest in the other person, value them and support them with problems.

Trust Rule No 10: Trust means believing another person, relying on them and interacting with them in an honest way.

Trust Rule No 11: Trust is learned behaviour that can reach back to childhood. We learn during life, and through experience, when it is right to trust, and when it is not.

Trust Rule No 12: Trustfulness has two components: self-trust (trust in our own skills) and trust in other people.

Trust Rule No 13: Trust is vital. Without a certain basic trust and trust in other people we would be lost.

Trust Rule No 14: Trust minimises complexity and makes our lives easier. For example, we can be more successful in business when we are trustworthy.

Trust Rule No 15: Trust and intimacy are two different things. All too often trust is mixed with intimacy. Trust is the catalyst for intimacy and fear is its natural enemy. Basically, intimacy is something that happens when two people feel close to each other.

Trust Rule No 16: We should always remember the saying, 'Healthy trust knows limits.' One should always know how far trust is acceptable.

Trust Rule No 17: Trust means admitting mistakes and taking responsibility for our mistakes.

Trust Rule No 18: Trust means being reliable. Someone who has trouble with punctuality and cannot meet deadlines forfeits trust.

Trust Rule No 19: Trust means being authentic and not playing a role. We should present ourselves the way we really are.

Trust Rule No 20: Trust means giving other people a chance, showing a leap of faith.

Trust Rule No 21: Trust always carries the risk of never knowing how a story ends. But it also offers the chance of a successful and happy life.

Download

Download your free e-book at

www.keypersonoftrust.de

This e-book delivers further inspiration for
becoming a Key Person of Trust.
Select Shop in the navigation bar and you will see a product:

FOR READERS OF MY BOOK:
Profit from a free e-book
Click on the product and order it free of charge.

The e-book will be sent to you after you have stated
this password when checking out (you may state
it as Additional Information in the menu):

KEYPERSONOFTRUST-INNERCIRCLE

Voices of Experts

To help you achieve maximum success with regard to trust, branding and entrepreneurship, and as a Key Person of Trust, I suggest you read the insights of other experts. The three following experts are highly respected influencers, and their expertise and opinions will help lead to your success. Read and learn what these experts have to say on their specialist topics:

- Branding: Denise Lee Yohn
- Marketing: Mark W Schaefer
- Influencer Marketing: Neal Schaffer

Before reading my interviews with these experts it is good to learn some facts first.

Definition of Branding

Branding is the process of giving meaning to a specific company, product or service by creating and shaping a brand in the mind of the consumer. It is a strategy designed by companies to help people quickly identify their products, services and organisation, and give them a reason to choose their products over the competition's, and clarifying, what this particular brand is and is not. The goal is

432

to attract and retain loyal customers by delivering a product that is always aligned with what the brand promises. Branding can be achieved in many ways:

- Visual identity of the brand (e.g. logo, website)
- Advertising and communication (e.g. flyers)
- Product and packaging design
- Experience in store
- Pricing
- Sponsoring and partnerships

'Branding is endowing products and services with the power of a brand' (Kotler & Keller, 2015). A brand is the perceived image of the product that is being sold, and branding is the strategy that achieves that image.

Definition of Marketing

According to Wikipedia: 'Marketing is defined by the American Marketing Association as "the activity, set of institutions, and processes for creating, communicating, delivering, and exchanging offerings that have value for customers, clients, partners, and society at large". The term developed from the original meaning, which referred literally to going to market with goods for sale. From a sales process engineering perspective, marketing is "a set of processes that are interconnected and interdependent with other functions" of a business aimed at achieving customer interest and satisfaction.

'The Chartered Institute of Marketing defines marketing as "the management process responsible for identifying, anticipating and satisfying customer requirements profitably".'

Marketing practice tended to be seen as a creative industry in the past. This included advertising, distribution and selling. However, the profession is now widely recognised as a science. The process of marketing involves bringing a product to market, which includes these steps:

- Broad market research
- Market targeting and market segmentation
- Determining distribution, pricing and promotion strategies
- Developing a communications strategy
- Budgeting
- Envisioning long-term market-development goals

According to *Business Dictionary*: 'Marketing is based on thinking about the business in terms of customer needs and their satisfaction. Marketing differs from selling, because (words of Harvard Business School's retired professor of marketing Theodore C Levitt) "Selling concerns itself with the tricks and techniques of getting people to exchange their cash for your product. It is not concerned with the values that the exchange is all about. And it does not, as marketing invariable does, view the entire business process as consisting of a tightly integrated effort to discover, create, arouse and satisfy customer needs."

'In other words, marketing has less to do with getting customers to pay for your product than developing a demand for that product and fulfilling the customer's needs.'

Definition of Influencer Marketing

According to Wikipedia: 'Influencer marketing is a form of marketing, in which focus is placed on influential people rather than the target market as a whole. It identifies the individuals that have influence over potential buyers, and orients marketing activities around these influencers.

'Influencer marketing tends to be broken into two sub-practices: earned influencer marketing and paid influencer marketing. Earned marketing stems from unpaid or pre-existing relationships with influencers or third-party content that is promoted by the influencer to further their own personal social growth. Paid influencer marketing campaigns can take the form of sponsorship, pre-roll advertising or testimonial messaging and can appear at any point in the content. Budgets vary widely and are usually based on audience reach.' Some marketers use influencer marketing to establish credibility in the market, others to create social conversations around their brand, others yet to drive online or in-store sales of their products.

'Influencer marketing derives its value from three sources: Social reach: Influencers are able to reach millions of consumers through their social channels and blogs. Original content: Influencers produce original, and oftentimes effective, marketing content for the brand. Consumer trust: Influencers maintain strong relationships with their audience, who have a certain level of trust in the influencer's opinions.

'Influencer marketing, in a commercial context, comprises four main activities: Identifying influencers, and ranking them in order of importance. Marketing to influencers, to increase awareness of the firm within the influencer community. Marketing through influencers, using influencers to increase market awareness of the firm amongst target markets. Marketing with influencers, turning influencers into advocates of the firm.'

Interview of Denise Lee Yohn on Branding

Denise Lee Yohn is the go-to expert on brand leadership for national media outlets in the United States, an in-demand speaker and consultant, and an influential writer. She is also the author of the bestselling book *What Great Brands Do: The Seven Brand-Building Principles that Separate the Best from the Rest* (Jossey-Bass), the e-book *Extraordinary Experiences: What Great Retail and Restaurant Brands Do*, and the new book *Fusion: How Integrating Brand and Culture Powers the World's Greatest Companies* (Nicholas Brealey/Hachette Books).

News media including FOX Business TV, CNBC, *The Wall Street Journal* and NPR call on Denise when they want an expert point of view on hot business issues. With her expertise and inspiring approach, Denise has become an in-demand keynote speaker. She has addressed business leaders around the world, including at The Art of Marketing in Toronto, EXPO Marketing in Mexico City, and Sustainable Brands in San Diego.

Denise enjoys challenging readers to think differently about brand-building in her regular contributions to *Harvard Business Review* and *Forbes*, and has been a sought-after writer for publications including *Fast Company*, *Entrepreneur*, *Knowledge@Wharton*, *Seeking Alpha* and *QSR Magazine*, among others.

Denise initially cultivated her brand-building approach through several high-level positions in advertising and client-side marketing. She served as lead strategist at advertising agencies for Burger King and Land Rover, and as the marketing leader and analyst for Jack in the Box restaurants and Spiegel catalogues. Denise went on to head Sony Electronic Inc.'s first brand office, where she was the vice president/general manager of brand and strategy and garnered major corporate awards. Consulting clients have included Target, Oakley, Dunkin' Donuts, and other leading companies.

Outside of her professional roles, Denise counts hiking Mount Kilimanjaro, dancing with a professional ballet company, and flying a helicopter as some of her greatest life experiences. Past speaking engagements:

- TEDx
- Cornell University
- Consumer Electronics Show
- Catalyst
- Lexus
- National Restaurant Show
- NFL
- Facebook
- The Conference Board

Media that has featured Denise:

- *New York Times*
- *CNBC*
- *Wall Street Journal*
- NPR
- *USA Today*
- *Harvard Business Review*
- *Advertising Age*
- *QSR Magazine*
- FOX Business TV

Denise's profile on LinkedIn: *www.linkedin.com/in/deniseleeyohn*
Denise's website: *deniseleeyohn.com*

Question 1

Your book, *What Great Brands Do*, discusses the seven brand-building principles that separate the best from the rest. It is said: 'Your brand is not what you say you are, it's what you do.' These seven brand-building principles as mentioned in your book:

1. Great brands start inside (they build a strong brand-led culture inside the organisation).
2. Great brands avoid selling products (it is all about developing emotional connections with customers instead of relying on product superiority).
3. Great brands ignore trends (they anticipate and interpret larger cultural movements).
4. Great brands don't chase customers (they embrace and celebrate what they stand for and accept that they are not for everyone).
5. Great brands sweat the small stuff (it is about designing your own customer experience to express your own brand values and attributes in the finest detail).
6. Great brands commit and stay connected (they concentrate fully on absolute brand aspirations and execute them relentlessly).
7. Great brands never have to 'give back' (they create shared value for all the stakeholders and always try to make a positive impact).

Summarised, that means that actions are the critical part of a brand, but what about a great profile, and presentation and communication? What about their role in brand building? How much significance do you see in these factors? What percentage does action play in brand building? Seventy percent? Ninety percent?

Denise's Answer

'Those elements, how you express your brand, are indeed very important, especially in today's environment, which is cluttered with lots of competing voices and efforts to gain people's attention. So you need to have effective communication and you need to stand out using your communication. But I think the problem that most companies have is that they overemphasise the importance of those external efforts. And they don't ground them and they don't make sure, before they express themselves, that they actually have a brand worth talking about. And so I would say that it's most important to make sure you have a strategic brand platform and that you are operationalising that platform. And then you can bring that to life through your presentation and communication.

'You asked me what percentage I would put on profile, presentation, and communication in brand building. I don't think it's really possible to quantify the percentage. I would say again that the order in which you undertake these things is more important. So work from the inside out and save your communication for when you're really clear about what you want to stand for and what you have to find as your brand.'

Question 2

Trust is one of the most critical components in building a strong and enduring brand. How can new companies and entrepreneurs build brand trust? Which factors are critical for success? On what factors should they concentrate? How can we become more trustworthy?

Denise's Answer

'The first thing is to make sure that you are clear on what is the value that you're creating and how you're going to deliver that value. So being focused and clear is critical and staying committed to that focus is critical, too, so that you end up delivering on what you say you're going to do.

'I think nothing destroys trust more than a company that promises to do great things and then breaks that promise or doesn't fulfil that promise. So I think the first thing is that you need to understand what promise you're going to make. And then you need to consistently deliver on that promise. You need to make sure that everything you do reflects the commitment and focus that you have.

'I also think aligning yourself with other brands or other institutions or other partners that may be more well established is a great way to signal that you are trustworthy. So, if you are providing a service, is there a complementary service that another well-established company offers that you can connect to? By showing that other companies, other organisations, are joining with you and want to work with you in your way can convey credibility to your customers. I think, though, the most important thing is to trust your customers.

'On being loyal to your customers, make sure you're doing what's in their best interest and that you are trusting first rather than expecting customers to give you the benefit of the doubt. I think the way to show that you are trustworthy is to trust your customers first and show them you trust them. So trust is a mutually enforcing relationship, as opposed to you proclaiming that you are trustworthy and expecting other people to believe you.'

Question 3

My book deals with branding as a Key Person of Trust. Such a person is characterised through 10 Key Qualities that should be developed if someone wants to be successful as a personality, leader and brand. These 10 Key Qualities are as follows:

1. Self-Trust + Self-Confidence
2. Authenticity/Credibility/Trustworthiness
3. Character + Attitude
4. Make a Difference/Know your Uniqueness + Distinctiveness
5. Learn to Present /Perform
6. Visibility/Attractiveness (for people, contacts and dream customers)
7. Develop a Personal Voice, Message, Mission and Vision
8. Create Chances + Opportunities/Get Orders easily
9. Good Reputation
10. More Trust + More Influence

How important do you consider these 10 Key Qualities are?

Denise's Answer

'I would say your points are very good. I would say all of them are important. A few stand out to me. Know how to make a difference/ know your uniqueness + distinctiveness is close to what I was talking about before. You really need to be clear about what you stand for. And that needs to be something that's different, distinctive and stands out. You need to play an irreplaceable role in people's lives. And then you need to make that uniqueness clear. Something that is critical.

'And I think, for a person increasing your self-trust and self-confidence is probably the first thing that you need to do because if you don't believe in yourself, you can't expect others to believe in you. So it's important that you're secure in yourself and believe in yourself well, before you expect other people to follow you.

'And finally, the one that kind of stuck out to me is develop your personal voice/message/mission/vision. I think if you were developing your personal brand having a purpose and values is critical. It might seem something that only larger organisations would need, but you as an individual need to have that clarity as well.'

Question 4

The success of a Key Person of Trust is based on four pillars: 1. Trust, 2. Personality, 3. Leadership and 4. Brand. How important do you consider a good personality and good leadership for the success of a brand?

Denise's Answer

'I'm guessing that you mean personality in terms of brand personality, which I would say is extremely important, because when I talk about brand personality, I think of the tone and manner and the kind of character with which the brand behaves and expresses itself. And those things can be highly differentiating for an organisation, or a product, or a service. Especially if the thing that you are selling is not as differentiated as your personality is. A good example would be one type of cereal that might be similar to another type of cereal, but the brand personality differentiates one from the other. So I would say that it is extremely important, but I would also warn that personality alone is not enough. You need a quality product and to provide good value.

'Good leadership is critically important for the success of a brand and the leaders in an organisation need to accept responsibility for building a brand. They can't delegate it to the marketing department or some other functional area. The top leaders of an organisation need to champion a brand and prioritize it and ensure that everyone in the organisation is aligned with it. So, I would say that personality and leadership are extremely important for the success of a brand.'

Question 5

Now let's talk about the definition of the terms 'brand' and 'branding'. Branding experts like Philip Kotler and Gary Armstrong say that brand is 'a name, term, sign, or symbol (or combination of these) that identifies the maker or seller of the product'. Marty Neumeier, however, says a brand is 'a person's gut feeling about a product, service, or organisation'. For me, a brand is a name with the power to influence, and branding is the process of giving a meaning to a specific company, of creating a business identity. What is a brand, and what does branding mean to you?

Denise's Answer

'A brand is, in basic terms, what you do and how you do it. The official business school definition of brand that I use is that your brand is the bundle of values and attributes that represent the value delivered to the customers and the way you do business. But essentially the shorthand version of the definition is that your brand is what you do and how you do it. And branding is the process of applying a visual and verbal identity to your brand so that your brand and values become associated with those visual and verbal identities. I don't like to talk about branding as the process of developing your brand because I think that short-sells, or undercuts, all that's involved in brand building. So I like to talk about brand building as in developing a powerful asset that creates value for you and your organisation.'

Question 6

What's next? What do you see as the future of branding? What trends are worth watching?

Denise's Answer

'Well, I would say, what's the future of brand building? And that to me has a lot to do with integration of internal culture and external brand identity. And that's why I wrote my most recent book, *Fusion: How Integrating Brand and Culture Powers the World's Greatest Companies*. I think that organisations are finding that their brand and their culture are not mutually enforcing and there isn't this interdependent relationship between the two. Also, it's a problem, whether it's not having the authenticity that customers and employees require, or whether it's wasting your efforts on brand building and/or culture building. And whether it's not having a healthy valuable culture and not having a differentiated brand. I think the thing that people are starting to pay more attention to, that will continue and should continue, is the alignment of the integration of brand and culture.

'The other kind of more tactical operational trend in brand building has to do with customer experience. And there has been a lot of work done on how to develop and design customer experience, which I think is really important. The element that I would add about work is that your customer experience needs to bring your brand to life; it's the embodiment of your brand. In many ways your customer experience is how people experience your brand and so you just don't want to have a good customer experience, you want to have an on-brand customer experience. So that's another direction, or another area, that people need to start focusing on. Because everyone is working on customer experience, so how you get ahead is by ensuring that you have a unique and differentiated customer experience, and that it is aligned with your brand.'

Interview of Mark W Schaefer on Marketing

Mark W Schaefer is a globally recognised blogger, speaker, educator, consultant and author who blogs at {grow}, one of the top marketing blogs in the world. As executive director of US-based Schaefer Marketing Solutions, he specialises in marketing strategy and social media workshops. Clients include both start-ups and global brands such as Adidas, J&J, Dell, AT&T, the United States Air Force, and the UK government. Mark has advanced degrees in marketing and organisational development, and holds seven patents. He is a faculty member of the graduate studies program at Rutgers University, and is the author of six bestselling books: *Social Media Explained*, *Return on Influence*, *Born to Blog*, *The Content Code*, *The Tao of Twitter* (four editions), and *Known: The Handbook for Building and Unleashing Your Personal Brand in the Digital Age*. His books have been translated into twelve languages and can be found in more than seven hundred libraries worldwide. He is the co-host of *The Marketing Companion*, one of the top ten marketing podcasts on iTunes.

In 2017 Mark was the seventh most-mentioned person by CMOs on Twitter and is among the top ten most re-tweeted marketing authorities in the world. He was listed as one of the top ten authorities on social selling by *Forbes*. He is among the world's most recognised social media authorities and has been a keynote speaker at conferences such as Social Media Week London, SXSW, National Economic Development Association, Word of Mouth Marketing Conference Tokyo, PR News, and the Institute for International and European Affairs. Mark has lectured at Oxford University, Princeton, and many other prestigious institutions.

Mark is a popular and entertaining commentator and has appeared on many national television shows in the United States, and has contributed to several periodicals, including the *Wall Street Journal*, *Wired* and *The New York Times*, and appeared on CNN, NPR, CNBC, the BBC and CBS NEWS. He is a regular contributing columnist to *The Harvard Business Review*.

Mark's profile on LinkedIn: *www.linkedin.com/in/markwschaefer*
Mark's website: *businessesgrow.com*

Question 1

Your book, *Known: The Handbook for Building and Unleashing Your Personal Brand in the Digital Age*, provides a step-by-step plan followed by most successful people in diverse careers like banking, education, real estate, construction, fashion and more. In today's world there is a permanent advantage to becoming known in our individual fields. Those who are known get the customers, the better jobs, and the invitations to exclusive opportunities. Today you must build an equity of influence by becoming known. How can we better become known?

Mark's Answer

'I did a tremendous amount of research and found that people who are known in their fields—around the world—all did the same four things to become known, without exception. First, you have to zero in on what you want to be known for. That is harder than it might seem. I write about establishing a 'sustainable interest'. This may or may not be the same as your passion, but it has to be something you can sustain for several years. Second, once you have your story, you have to find a place to tell it, hopefully an under-served niche. In the book I have exercises to help you identify that. Third, you have to find a way to tell that story through some sort of content. This is where a lot of people get lost. But I encourage people to choose one channel—written, video, audio or visual—and stick to it. Finally, you have to build an actionable audience, which is different from a social media audience, which is generally weak relational links. This takes consistent effort, but it does work over time.'

Question 2

Trust is one of the most critical components in building a strong and enduring brand. How can new companies and entrepreneurs build brand trust?

Mark's Answer

'There is a good chance that they can't. If you look at the facts, trust in companies, brands and advertising has declined for ten years in a row. Even if you're doing a good job and telling the truth, people still probably don't believe you. While people don't trust companies, they do trust people, especially experts and entrepreneurs. This is why personal branding is so important. In the past, our businesses and brands were built through an accumulation of advertising impressions, but in the future they will be built through an accumulation of human impressions. Building personal brands builds trust.'

Question 3

You are an expert on marketing. Marketing is the process of getting consumers interested in a company's products or services. Marketing is about determining the value of a product or service, and communicating that information to the customer. Marketing is used to create, keep and satisfy the customer. How would you define the word marketing?

Mark's Answer

'Marketing is responsible for all the activities involved in creating demand for a product or service.'

Interview of Neal Schaffer on Influencer Marketing

In addition to being named one of marketing's ten biggest thought leaders by CMO.com, Neal Schaffer has been recognised as a *Forbes* top fifty social media power influencer, and a *Forbes* top five social sales influencer. Neal Schaffer is a leading authority on helping businesses through their digital transformation of sales and marketing through consulting, training, and helping enterprises, large and small, develop social media marketing strategy, influencer marketing, and social selling initiatives. President of the social media agency PDCA Social, Neal also teaches digital media to executives at Rutgers University, the Irish Management Institute (Ireland), and the University of Jyvaskyla (Finland).

Fluent in Japanese and Mandarin Chinese, Neal is a popular keynote speaker and has been invited to speak about digital media on four continents in a dozen countries. He is also the author of three books on social media, including *Maximize Your Social*, and in 2019 will publish his fourth book, *The Business of Influence*, which focuses on educating the market on the why and how every business should leverage the potential of influencer marketing.

In addition to the above, Neal is creator of the leading social media for business blog, *Maximize Social Business*, co-founder of the social media industry's definitive social media conference, the Social Tools Summit, and founder of the soon-to-be-launched Social Media Center of Excellence, to build and educate a community surrounding best practices in using social media for business. Neal resides in Irvine, California, but also travels frequently to Japan.

Neal's profile on LinkedIn: *www.linkedin.com/in/nealschaffer*
Neal's website: *nealschaffer.com*

Question 1

Your book, *The Business of Influence: How Anyone Can Plug Their Business into the Influencer Economy and Achieve Massive Results*, teaches how to leverage influencer marketing for our own business and ourselves. Influencer marketing is trending upwards and businesses are able to benefit from it. Businesses can leverage influencer marketing to spread their message to millions of people. Studies confirm that collaborating with social media influencers to produce, distribute and promote sponsored content is now one of the most powerful ways for brands to reach consumers. Influencer marketing must be a core component of a company's overall business objectives. What about a great profile, a great presentation and great communication? How significant do you see these factors? How can we better connect with influencers?

Neal's Answer

'I am not sure if you are asking this question from a brand or personal perspective. I do believe that in order to yield influence, whether you are a person or a company, you need to have a specific objective or *raison d'etre*. For brands, this will be to sell products and services. For professionals, it will vary. Armed with an objective, your influence will actually depend on your profile (= branding), your presentation (= publication of content related to your objective on a regular basis), and being a great communicator (= engaging with your followers and the general community of potential followers). So yes, they are all significant.

'As to how one can better connect with influencers, I talk about this in my upcoming book, but it really comes down to genuine engagement and treating influencers with respect. Before asking them to collaborate with you, first pay it forward and offer to help them. I have an entire chapter in *The Business of Influence* on how to engage with influencers, so it is hard to answer in a few sentences, but hopefully this helps.'

Question 2

Trust is one of the most critical components for building a strong and enduring brand. How can new companies and entrepreneurs build brand trust? Which factors are critical for success? How can we become more trustworthy?

Neal's Answer

'Trust is one of the most important concepts in business and life. We only want to become friends with, and do business with, entities that we truly trust. For new companies and entrepreneurs, it will unfortunately take time to build trust, as trust can only be built over time through repetitive engagements. The beauty about social media is that it allows brands and entrepreneurs to be seen by many people repeatedly, as they become more engaged in social media. Paid social and influencer marketing only accelerate this process. There is a famous quote from Woody Allen that I am quite fond of: 'Ninety percent of success is showing up.' Social media gives brands the opportunity to build trust by having a consistent presence and creating relationships with others.'

Question 3

My book deals with branding as a Key Person of Trust. Such a person is characterised through 10 Key Qualities that should be developed if someone wants to be successful as a personality, leader and brand. These 10 Key Qualities are as follows:

1. Self-Trust + Self-Confidence
2. Authenticity/Credibility/Trustworthiness
3. Character + Attitude
4. Make a Difference/Know your Uniqueness + Distinctiveness
5. Learn to Present/Perform
6. Visibility/Attractiveness (for people, contacts and dream customers)

7. Develop a Personal Voice, Message, Mission and Vision
8. Create Chances + Opportunities/Get Orders easily
9. Good Reputation
10. More Trust + More Influence

How important do you consider these 10 Key Qualities are? How can we increase our influence?

Neal's Answer

'I think that all of these are extremely important. There isn't one that I would change. Obviously, from a trust perspective, a leadership perspective, a branding perspective, certain of these ten qualities will be more important than others, but I believe a combination of these will allow one to gain trust and influence. As far as influence is specifically concerned, I believe that the most important qualities from the above list are:

- Authenticity/Credibility/Trustworthiness
- Make a Difference/Know your Uniqueness + Distinctiveness
- Learn to Present/Perform
- Develop a Personal Voice, Message, Mission and Vision
- Visibility/Attractiveness
- Good Reputation

'I would say that the first four are necessary for the base of building influence, while achieving visibility, increasing attractiveness, and developing a good reputation are essential in order to increase one's influence.'

Question 4

The success of a Key Person of Trust is based on four pillars: 1. Trust, 2. Personality, 3. Leadership and 4. Brand. How important do you consider a good personality and good leadership for the success of a brand?

Neal's Answer

'This is an interesting question. There are many successful brands, for whom the average consumer doesn't even know who the leader of the brand is. However, as our relationships with our employers continue to be redefined and there is a greater focus on employee engagement, I believe that those brands with good personality or culture, as well as good leadership, will, over time, have a better success of attracting better talent and retaining them longer.'

Question 5

You are an expert on influencer marketing. Influence is being able to affect an action. When we are able to alter, inspire or change someone's behaviour we have influenced them. Influence is the key to success. To me, a brand is a name with the power to influence. Having influence within our social relationships has many benefits and can help to further our careers. How would you define the word influence? Why is having influence so important? And what is an influencer to you? Should we all try to become influencers?

Neal's Answer

'Yes, influence is the sway that a person, brand or thing has over someone that can induce them to action. Influence is important on many levels. If you want to become a Key Person of Trust, having influence will greatly help you achieve that. Yielding influence will also help brands and professionals in achieving whatever it is they want. This is why I recommend that everybody should try to yield more influence in their industry, company, or even community. Those with influence are often those with decision-making opportunities and thus can better influence the outcome of matters that might be vital to them.'

Question 6

What's next? What do you see as the future for the topics of influence and influencer marketing? Which trends will be worth watching?

Neal's Answer

'I believe that influencer marketing has just begun. Companies will begin to realise that organic social media marketing is all but dead, and it will be more efficient and lucrative to team up with influencers to get the job done. This is one of the major trends that I see continuing for some time, and thus I am invested in writing a book and speaking on the subject.'

Implementing What You Have Learned

Good branding is a personal agenda. The hardest thing for leaders to understand and execute is a strategy that requires important changes in human behaviour. We cannot begin by simply thinking differently. When we want to be successful, we must also implement what we have learned, which means acting in a new way.

It's up to you now. Consolidate what you have learned. Implement the things you have learned in this book, and your life will change. Learn from the book and work out your success. Do something for your personal branding. Develop trust, and your personality, leadership and brand further. Become a Key Person of Trust.

References

I have used the following sources in my research:

'The Importance of Relationships in Business', Better Business Bureau
'Building Trust Across Cultures', Erin Meyer
Trust … the Only Kind of Influence That Really Matters, Karin Sebelin
'4 Ways to Define Trust in the New World of Work', Meghan M Biro
'The Concept of Trust', Springer
'15 Facts about Trust: Definition, Types and Perspectives', Accolade
   Communications
'What is Trust?' Changing Minds
'Know Me, Like Me, Trust Me', Karin Sebelin
'On the Importance of Trust in Business', DZone
'Why Trust is a Critical Success Factor For Businesses Today', YEC
The Speed of Trust, Stephen MR Covey
'4 Reasons Why Trust is NOT Earned', Maggie Rowe
'Is your Mindset Sabotaging Your Success?' Erin Olivo, PhD
'16 Ways Leaders Kill Trust', Skip Prichard
Making Ethical Decisions, Josephson Institute of Ethics (e-book)
'4 Questions to Build Trust and Have Your Expectations Met', Dennis Reina
'Maslow's Hierarchy of Needs', Saul McLeod
'How Do You Recognize a Trustworthy Leader?' Linda Fischer Thornton
'The Law of Respect: Trust Starts with Respect', Karin Sebelin
'17 Verbal Habits of Highly Likable People', Bill Murphy

The New Relationship Marketing, Mari Smith

The Courage to Trust: A Guide to Building..., Cynthia Lynn Wall (LCSW)

'Mehr Selbstvertrauen. Mehr Erfolg', Karin Sebelin

'Five Steps to Increase Your Influence', Susan Tardanico

Act Like a Leader, Think Like a Leader, Herminia Ibarra

'How to Increase Your Influence at Work', Rebecca Knight

Lead 4 Success: Learn the Essentials of True Leadership, George Hallenbeck

Becoming a Person of Influence, John C Maxwell

The 21 Irrefutable Laws of Leadership, John C Maxwell

'Classical Rhetoric 101: The Three Means of Persuasion', Brett and
    Kate McKay

'Influence', Chambers and Associates Pty Ltd

'40 Ways to Self-Promote Without Being a Jerk', Bruce Kasanoff

'Building Relationships: 11 Rules for Self-Promotion', Dustin Wax

'How to Sell to 4 Different Personality Types', Aja Frost

Steal the Show, Michael Port

'The Science of Selling Yourself: 3 Nonverbal Ways to Gain Trust', Bernie Reeder

'10 Things You Can Do to Boost Self-Confidence', Chris W. Dunn

'The Extraordinary Power of Visualising Success', Matt Mayberry

'Brand Story', Bernadette Jiwa

'7 Habits That Make Great Opportunities Happen', Liz Strauss

'6 Ways to Differentiate Yourself to Beat Your Competitor', Mark Hunter

'The Aim of Marketing is to Make Selling Superfluous', Karin Sebelin

'Slogans vs Taglines: What is your Brand's Battlecry?' Laura Ries

'15 Ways to Be a Highly Remarkable Person', Kyle Robbins

*The LinkedIn Playbook: Contacts to Customers. Engage. Connect.
    Convert*, Adam Houlahan

'What is Influence and How to Have It', InNetwork

'What Marketers Should Know About Personality-Based Marketing',
    Christopher Graves and Sandra Matz

'What Buddha Knew About the Law of Attraction', Boni Lonnsburry

Man's Search for Meaning, Viktor E. Frankl

'How to be an 'Overnight Success', Gary Vaynerchuck

'Blue Ocean Strategy: Creating Your Own Market', Carlyann Edwards

'10 Tips on How to Become a Thought Leader', Matt Sweetwood

Die Zeit der smarten Experten, Brigitte and Ehrenfried Conta Gromberg

'The Lesson in Economics That 80000 Businesses Never Learned',
    David Brier

'5 Powerful Types of Influencers to Woo Your Audience Today', The
    Storyteller Marketer

'A study on human behaviour has identified four basic personality
    types', the Universidad Carlos III de Madric (UC3M)

About the Author

KARIN SEBELIN is the author of two German children's books, co-author of a German anthology, and author of several books about trust, ethical leadership and branding. She is a trust expert and personal branding coach for Becoming a Key Person of Trust.

An entrepreneur since 2011, Karin coaches (beginning) entrepreneurs with a new branding concept based on four pillars: 1. Trust, 2. Personality, 3. Leadership, and 4. Brand, and helps them become remarkable personalities, great leaders, and trusted and respected brands, and achieve maximum success.

Karin Sebelin considers trust the foundation of happiness. As CEO of Presse-Service Karin Sebelin, as freelance journalist, editor, writer and communications consultant, she made her first acquaintance with the topic of trust.

Through business networking on Ecademy (August 2011 until July 2012), Karin learned much about tolerance, trust and collaboration. She had great success in this network. People loved her blogs and work very much, and for many weeks she ranked as number one among the 600,000 members of this network in the Ecademy Score.

Karin lives with her husband and their two sons in Friolzheim, Germany.

Contact Karin:

info@karinsebelin.com

Visit Karin's blogs:

keypersonoftrust.de

karinsebelin.com

Connect with Karin:

Twitter: @KarinSebelin

Instagram: karinsebelin

Facebook: www.facebook.com/karinsebelin

LinkedIn: www.linkedin.com/in/karinsebelin/?locale=en_US

Thank You

I am grateful that you have been interested enough to read my book. I want to offer you some opportunities. I regularly write interesting newsletters for my readers, so if you would like to be on the mailing list to receive tips, ideas and news from the world of trust, entrepreneurship and branding, subscribe to my branding newsletter 'Branding Messages'. Stay up to date, get inspirations for your success, and benefit from my expertise.

- To receive the newsletter, subscribe here: www.keypersonoftrust. de/newsletter
- To follow my blog and read my articles, go to: www. keypersonoftrust.de
- You will receive a reward if you write a review of this book. Here's how you can do that:

1. Write a review of this book.
2. Post the review on Amazon, or alternatively post it on your blog, on your Facebook page, or have it published in another publication.
3. Send the link to your post or a screenshot to info@karinsebelin.com.
4. As a gift, I will send you interesting invitations, and opportunities to enjoy coaching and various products at a reduced price.

Thank you for your trust and time. If you liked the book, you may certainly recommend it further.

Also by Karin Sebelin

Trust ... the Only Kind of Influence That Really Matters can be ordered as a paperback or Kindle edition through Amazon.com, Amazon.co.uk, Amazon.de, worldwide or via CreateSpace.

The Ethical Entrepreneur can be ordered as a Kindle edition through Amazon.com, Amazon.co.uk, Amazon.de, and worldwide.

THE ETHICAL
ENTREPRENEUR:

A Workbook for Ethical Leadership

10 Key Elements for Success

Karin Sebelin

Persönlichkeitsentwicklung – Erfolgsfaktor Vertrauen: Grundlagen – Hintergründe – Strategien can be ordered as a Kindle edition through Amazon.com, Amazon.co.uk, Amazon.de, and worldwide.

CPSIA information can be obtained
at www.ICGtesting.com
Printed in the USA
BVHW041338010519
547057BV00029B/1815/P

9 783000 606526